I0102905

BOUGHT LESSONS

A Bought Lesson
Is a Learned Lesson

SYLVIA M. GATES

Revised Edition

Copyright © 2020 Sylvia M. Gates.

All rights reserved. No part of this book may be used or reproduced by any means, graphic, electronic, or mechanical, including photocopying, recording, taping or by any information storage retrieval system without the written permission of the author except in the case of brief quotations embodied in critical articles and reviews.

This book is a work of non-fiction. Unless otherwise noted, the author and the publisher make no explicit guarantees as to the accuracy of the information contained in this book and in some cases, names of people and places have been altered to protect their privacy.

This book has been REVISED to make corrections to details important to the veracity of the author's story. Due to the dynamics of the Internet. web addresses or links may change.

This REVISED EDITION book can be ordered on amazon.com.

Published by Sylvia M. Gates
Irmo. South Carolina 29063
www.sylviamgatesmm.store
sylviasbook14@yahoo.com

Scripture references from the King James Version of the bible. (KJV)

Cover photo by: Arlene Gates
Cover color idea: LaDoris B. Walker

Paperback ISBN# 978-0-578-76084-1
Kindle /eBook ISBN# 978-0-578-76085-8

DEDICATION

To My Parents,
Andrew and Lillian Gates
To my dad and mom, Andrew and Lillian Gates. You are the best.
Thank you for birthing me into a family of great faith. Thank you
for the moral values you instilled in me. Thank you even for the
times I thought you were too strict. You model love and faith, and
your model of God's love gives me the fortitude to persist. Because
of you, I can look adversity in the eye and fight. I can't thank
God enough for you two. It is to you that I dedicate this book.

In Memory of My Spiritual Parents,
Andrew and Carrie Freeman
To Mr. and Mrs. Andrew and Carrie Freeman for providing
me a place for Bible study. You counseled me and countless
other young Christians. Your home was our happy place,
where we could go for yummy food and even better spiritual
food. You modeled God's love and acceptance. May you rest
in peace as we await Jesus's triumphant return. Thank you.

CONTENTS

Acknowledgments

For more than twenty-five years, that "still small voice," as described by the prophet Elijah in 1 King 19:11–12, has admonished me to write. I made many starts over the years but was repeatedly sidetracked. I diverted my energies to what at that moment seemed to be a more urgent task. Repeatedly, I responded to the voice that quietly whispered, "Write," only to start another unfinished product. I understood that it was the voice of God instructing me to write my story. I wanted to obey Him, but the task was too great. I had to visit some hurtful places, places that made me want to run away. Run away, I did. I am now writing my story as I recall it.

Just recently, I celebrated my seventieth birthday on a cruise to the western Caribbean. Realizing that most of my life was behind me, I knew that I must obey God and tell my story before I depart from this earth. Now that I am seventy, I am faced with additional challenges. I suffer from double vision, which increases with stress. My memory is a challenge. And revisiting past hurts are as real now as they were on that terrible night almost fifty years ago.

I surrendered my time and my will and started writing. I must acknowledge that when I started writing, I found myself in another room, surfing television channels, just doing anything in order to avoid the past that has penalized me all these years.

I thank God for His guidance in this work. I thank Him for not only living among us today but for loving us enough. No, for loving *me* enough. I thank Him for being so concerned that He would intervene in the life of an ordinary person such as myself to help ordinary people such as you. Thank you, Cedelle Gates, for your offer to help with the editing and to my beautiful daughter, Kristen, thanks for reminding me of the importance of telling my story. The two of you took away my excuses when I was overwhelmed with the magnitude of the task I faced.

Thank you to my friend Rose Parkman Marshall, a published author, for encouraging me to persevere. Thank you for editing my first work and for your expert advice. Thanks to my cousin Janice Dinkins for taking the time to read the information and enthusiastically encouraging me to continue. Thanks to my cousin Arlene Gates for her artistic insight, and to my friends Lynn Mines and Pat Harrison for their input.

Thank you to Deborah Anderson, my brother Ronald Gates and his altruistic wife, Sheila, for their technical help. Temeka Blackwell, I appreciate the way you traveled to support my efforts. Zenobia, you were my voice of reason. Plus, you embody organization and management. It kept me grounded during the writing process. All of you gave me the insight and the encouragement I needed to tackle this difficult task despite my physical and emotional difficulties.

I am also grateful to the many youtube.com artists whose songs comforted me as I wrote. They helped me push through the pain. It was not easy, but you helped me push through, and I appreciate you.

Introduction

Learning without thought is labor lost;
thought without learning is perilous.
CONFUCIUS

"Tell me and I'll forget; show me and I may remember; involve me and I'll understand," is the old Chinese proverb that caught my attention when I taught high school students with learning challenges. I painted it permanently on the walls of my classroom in order to help students understand that true learning required active participation. I did not realize that the proverb was a self-fulfilling prophecy in my life. God was my teacher in the classroom of life. He taught me many lessons through experience. They were hard lessons. Yes, I bought these lessons. Mama said a bought lesson is a learned lesson.

I share my life experiences with the hopes that each reader will develop a similar personal relationship with our Lord Jesus, as I have. He was the One who saved me and taught me these all-important lessons. It is my prayer that the devotions included in this book will provide you guidance on how you can develop the strength and fortitude necessary to live this life victoriously through unwavering faith in Jesus—even when you are in the depths of your personal trials and tribulations.

Year after year, God instructed me to write. Unfortunately,

I could not face the painful memories embedded in me. You see, I had buried those painful memories deep inside and built an emotional brick wall. It hurt too much to deal with. When asked what happened to me, it was just easier to say I was involved in an auto accident. After that lie, I would quickly change the subject. It was the 1970s, and being shot was not supposed to happen to good people. Or at least that is what everyone else believed. Yes, I was embarrassed about what others would think if I told them I was shot. My parents always told me to "be a good girl," and what people thought of me was important to them, and therefore by extension, me. Writing forced me to face that tragedy that I wanted so desperately to forget, even though the paralysis on the left side remained a taunting reminder.

Ten years ago, I made an unsuccessful attempt at writing an e-book after I finally paid heed to His instructions. That was the therapy I desperately needed. I prayed, asking God to provide me with someone to help me write. When He did not respond, I realized that I could no longer wait for someone to come along and physically help me. This was my burden to lift, and I had to do it on my own. I am now putting my aching, overused, arthritic right hand's fingers on the keyboard to share the lessons God has taught me. Finally, my soul is ready to expose itself to the world. I offer no pretense of being super strong; I chose to expose my humanity in an effort to show that life has its ups and downs. Proverbs 24:16 describes my struggle. I got discouraged, I wanted to give up, but I learned to trust God to help me get up and try again. It is my prayer and hope that your life will be enriched and changed as you journey through the lessons I bought. Mama is right. A bought lesson is a learned lesson.

POW! POW! POW!

Our greatest weakness lies in giving up. The most certain
way to succeed is always to try just one more time.

THOMAS EDISON

Pow, pow, pow invaded my otherwise peaceful sleep last night. That
is the reason I keep the mementos from my past near my bed. I
have learned to encourage myself. My parents continue to remind
me that it is wrong to "brag on oneself" and that "compliments are
something other people are supposed to give you." I found out the
hard way that it is easier for people to pull you down and point out
shortcomings than to compliment you. The disparaging remarks
made it more difficult to adjust to the limitations and daily struggles
I faced.

That reminds me, I was evaluated by a psychologist about
twenty-five years ago, when I realized that after twenty-plus years
of working while paralyzed, I could not struggle another day. I
sought out a therapist because I was falling apart. I thought I was
having a breakdown. He assured me, however, that if I were having
a breakdown, I'd think everyone else around me was having a
breakdown, but I would never think that of myself. Wow! Was

1

that freeing! His evaluation of me was impressive. I made quite an impression on him and that boosted my self-esteem.

Can you imagine what it was like to the ego to have to stop work at age forty-five? Imagine having an alert and capable mind but a body that was hurting and worn out from pushing itself to compete with able-bodied people. And I did compete! The playing field was not equal, but I was accustomed to playing on an uneven field. I'm black, and I'm a woman! Hey, I learned how to "fight like a girl."

The psychologist was impressed at how I defied all odds and worked despite my physical problems. I believe that he was even more impressed that my greatest struggle was the desire to continue to work. I was well trained; I loved my profession. I fought to continue to work even though I was paralyzed in the left hand and quickly losing the use of my right hand due to overuse syndrome. I literally had no hands that worked, yet I wanted to work. That was my identity. That was how I got my respect. I was a teacher! I did not want to lose my class.

The psychologist stated that my biggest problem was I received too much negative feedback. I did not have enough positivity or enough praise. But now that I think about it, I live with a disability, and society is conditioned to look at the "dis" rather than the "ability." Society's treatment was, in many ways, more paralyzing than my left hand, which felt pain yet was lifeless. Attitudes were more paralyzing than the paralysis.

I am a proud black woman with strong faith and family values. I'm a survivor. I have been down the road of hard knocks, and I have done what I needed to do to rise above my plight. I am a survivor. But for the first time, I am telling it like it is. With God's help, I did life; I am doing life. My truth is life was and is hard, yet it is real. I must daily encourage myself to persist. With God's help, I am doing life. Below is my experience. I bought these lessons.

I awake the next morning a bit disturbed and sad for no apparent reason. Suddenly, I feel a little shaky, a bit snappy. I feel sad, just plain sad. The next day is Thanksgiving. My mom is the best cook, and my dad is the greatest turkey carver. As always, the food is festive and yummy. Dad had smoked the turkey to perfection. Mom made the giblet gravy with boiled eggs and all. The collards are sliced almost paper-thin and overcooked to perfection. Although she uses olive oil to season instead of pork, it is unbelievably good. I usually make a sweet potato casserole and maybe string bean casserole and lima beans. My two brothers' wives also bring special dishes. We have the usual feast, with everybody chattering and scurrying around. But I go through the motions because I had to take a pill just to make it through the day.

It does not end with Thanksgiving. This depression is a "gift" that keeps on taking. After Thanksgiving comes Christmas. I just want to get the holidays over with. For the joy of my child, I went through the motions. However, after she was grown and gone, it became the same as Thanksgiving. I had to take pills to get through Christmas too.

Nope, these are not pleasure pills, although I heard news reports that addicts robbed places to get these pills. I can't imagine anyone taking the stuff for pleasure. We know that there is no pleasure in being an addict. Now don't get me wrong, I don't abuse the pills. My physician once commented that I am not the personality who would abuse the medication. How true. I hate taking medicine. I hate the way this stuff makes me feel. But during these holidays, it is my key to survival. I'm sedated just enough to be able to show up and go through the motions. Often, I don't remember all the details. I am sedated enough to go through the motions of life.

I am so sad. It has nothing to do with the fact that people get depressed in the winter due to light deprivation because of the short days. I am sad because most of the time, I wish I had died on that Thanksgiving Eve forty-eight years ago. I'm sad because I know that to end my life would hurt my wonderful parents and my precious daughter, who is an only child. My parents are elderly, and my daughter would virtually be alone. Her daddy, my ex-husband? Well, that's another story of survival! And I do mean a survival story, but I'll save it for another book.

Why the sadness? It is called post-traumatic stress disorder (PTSD). Yes, post-traumatic stress disorder. When I let my guard down, it gets the best of me. It always attacks me in November. But I know how to pull myself up. I get in the Word. That's the Bible—my rock, my sanity.

Shortly after my injury, my doctor prescribed Valium while explaining that I'd have to take it for the rest of my life. Huh? I did not like the way it made me feel. I think it is what folks describe as high. Thank God I later found a better high, one that does not leave me sleepy or impair my thinking; a high that never makes me feel low. I invited Christ into my life, and He helped me through those horrible times of memories and the repercussions of a traumatic brain injury. Let me explain. It did not erase the PTSD or memories of the trauma, but it helped me survive those horrifying and potentially debilitating times in my life. I am forever grateful for God's Word and the peace it affords. That is the key to my sanity.

2

DISRUPTED TRANSITION

And the prayer of faith will save the sick, and the Lord will raise
him up; and if he has committed sins, they shall be forgiven him.

JAMES 5:15

I died on November 24, 1971. I was literally present at my death. I
was strangely aware of what was happening to my body. It was a cool
Wednesday night when I *felt* it in the cool rush of my spirit. I can't
think of any way to describe it other than an out-of-body experience.
I was conscious throughout the process. And I felt my soul move,
transitioning toward the light, which signaled the beginning of the
great beyond.

However, my transition was abruptly interrupted. The prayers
of my parents and community successfully touched God's heart.
He yanked me out of my transition and sent me back to them. My
spirit—my breath—returned to my body as it lay in the operating
room of the newly desegregated Columbia Hospital. As the heart
rate monitor beeped back to life, a black nurse in the operating room
insisted the doctors persevere in their efforts to resuscitate me. I am
told that she would not let them give up on me, even though it had
been a while since the heart rate monitor had flatlined. My family's

5

and community's prayers were evidently directing the actions and judgments of the medical professionals treating me.

Resuscitated, I now lay praying. I heard the harmonious lyrics of the hymn "Precious Lord"—"Precious Lord, take my hand, lead me on, let me stand"—fill the room. The song intended for my funeral was instead my emotional plea to God to take my living hand and lead me on. God fortunately heard our prayers and fulfilled them. God put my life back in my body. Once I was fully conscious, I was so thankful to be alive. Yet I was simultaneously embarrassed.

I had been shot! Shot like a common criminal. That was not supposed to happen to me. I always tried to do what was right. I made sure I treated people right. I went to church, and no matter what, I followed the rules of God and society, making sure I never hurt anyone intentionally or unintentionally. I must confess, I did occasionally speed on the highway. But whenever I was caught, I dutifully paid the ticket. Eventually, I even gave up that habit and resolved to be more careful.

Getting shot is something that is supposed to happen to rowdy, unruly people. Or so I thought. I distinctly remembered hearing reports and stories of stabbings and shootings being frequent among people who lived *that* kind of life. I was no robber baron. So why was I here on this operating table? *Now what will my grandparents think of me?* I wondered.

As I gradually came to my senses, I realized I was in the intensive care unit (ICU). I asked about my ear's condition as a bullet had hit my right ear. A shocked silence befell the room. From the looks on the faces of the small group of doctors surrounding me in my hospital bed, I could tell everyone was surprised I was still alert, and my mind was intact. A nurse broke the silence by asking me if I were a nurse because I was using medical jargon when I questioned them about my ear.

I sighed and explained that I was trained in speech pathology and audiology. At that moment, I was intrigued to know about the state of my ear, so much so that I wanted to examine it to see the damage for myself. As I tried to lift my left arm to do that, I realized I could not. My left side was totally paralyzed. When I informed the doctors of this, they poked me with pens along my left side and asked me if I felt them. As they did this, I noticed the doctor was smiling. I thought he was not taking my condition seriously, and this irritated me.

In my usual brash manner, I asked the doctor why he was constantly smiling at me. Although I was thankful to be alive, I still felt that there was nothing in intensive care to smile about, especially when I could not feel the entire left side of my body. With his smile never breaking, the doctor replied, "You better be glad I have something to smile about." I understood that the doctor was smiling because of my miraculous recovery. I smiled, too, and did not complain anymore.

For the next few days, I spent my time recovering in the ICU ward. Now that I was back to life, I had learned that sometimes— no, oftentimes—bad things happen to good people. I had not done anything wrong, yet I was shot, nonetheless. But God! While it had almost cost me my life through that near-death experience, I now have the assurance that God is indeed real. God is alive. God is effective in our lives today, at this moment. My death was not the end but only the beginning of the many lessons God taught me through this one incident. I had to die to buy the lesson that prayer works. Indeed, these lessons almost cost my life. Moreover, they were extremely hard lessons that wore me down physically and mentally. However, with hindsight being 20/20, I can comfortably say that most of the time, it was worth it.

I was moved to a semi-private room. The bed next to me was occupied by a young girl who was in her teens. Although my eyes were bandaged and I could not see her, her voice made it likely that she was a teenager. In any case, she was a quiet girl who spent most of her time engrossed in the numerous books on her bedside table, reading them out loud. Her mother visited her daily to check with her on how her recovery was progressing. Then early in one morning, I awoke to the shrill cries of her mother. Nurses rushed into the room as her mother cried for a doctor. At first, I could not make out what all the commotion was about, but as it unfolded before me, I realized what happened. The little girl had passed away. Her mother was wailing over the loss of her precious daughter.

A few days after this, her mother returned to the empty bed next to mine to collect her deceased daughter's belongings. We had never spoken much with each other, but I could tell that her child's death was still haunting her mind. We spoke for a bit, mainly discussing the behavior of her daughter, until silence befell us. Now that I knew for sure that God existed, I broke the silence between us and said to her with a strong conviction in my voice, "She is with the Lord." I do not know how much that helped her, but I noticed the creases on her face soften.

3

TRAGEDY

I must be taken as I have been made. The success is not mine,
the failure is not mine, but the two together make me.

CHARLES DICKENS

It was November. Winter would officially arrive in just a few weeks, but the air was already becoming chilly. Lying in bed, I yawned and stretched as I turned over toward the television. After watching a few of the headlines, my eyes focused on the silver bowl placed on the coffee table with my name etched around the rim, along with my retirement date and the name of the high school where I was last employed. I slowly trailed my eyes along the wall to a framed pair of Maurice Utrillo prints. One of them had an orange inscription on its bottom left corner, written there by the colleague who printed and gifted the prints to me. I squinted at the inscription in hopes of clearing my vision to read the printed inscription, but it was in vain.

I smiled as I wondered, *why am I trying to fool myself?* I know that life for me began at forty. *It begin to break down, and my eyesight was the first to go.* I fished for my glasses around the base of the bed, where I usually put them. I quickly found them and put them on, reading the orange inscription with pride. The paintings were presented to me when I left my teaching position in Ft. Worth, Texas. On one of the two paintings, it reads, "To a teacher with a heart as big as Texas." I always laughed at that as I thought of the many young people whom I taught during my twenty-plus years as an educator of special needs children and adults. It was hard work, but I had taught them and loved them as I struggled to overcome my own adversities. Nah, I take that back. Adversity does not adequately describe my life. I ought to use words like "misfortune," "calamity," "hardship," or "struggle."

You see, I am a proud woman who is the survivor of domestic violence. There are no words in the dictionary to describe what my life has been like. I had to learn to lean on Jesus. My life might have been unbearable except for my sustaining faith in Jesus Christ. That is the only way I survived the nightmares, the disappointments, the prejudice, and the unfair treatment that I have endured as a result of what someone did to me, someone I thought was my best friend. He should have wanted to protect me. Love protects. Love does not hurt or harm. The mere thought of that kind of betrayal is devastatingly painful to my self-esteem. I don't claim to be a saint. I stressed so much that it affected me physically. I would not have survived if not for my faith in God. It was with bulldog tenacity that I chose to trust God when all else seemed impossible.

The paintings were my avenue of escape to the good ole days. Good old days? There was not a lot of good in those old days as far as I can recall. Those were the days when I was so exhausted that I had little to no energy, yet somehow I managed to keep my head above water long enough to go to work each day, so I could provide for myself and my young daughter. Those years are now long gone, but for some reason, that morning, I allowed my mind to reflect on those bittersweet years. I took inventory of the evidence, proving that the challenges I faced were indeed real and that I had something tangible to represent those years spent in the classroom, where I held professional certification in two states. I lovingly taught children with speech and learning disabilities as I struggled to manage my own life. Life indeed was a struggle, but I enjoyed my job and loved parenting my beautiful little girl alongside teaching all those precious children.

Let me go back. Let me walk down a path that had overgrown in my mind and spirit. Let me travel a path littered with memories, has-beens, and pain. Please walk with me for a few minutes. I must confess that my heart hurts, and I experience severe anxiety. I cry deeply as I painfully recall these memories.

It was a typical southeastern autumn day, not very cold yet slightly windy. The rains had finally stopped, and there was a chill hanging in the air that could be felt right in the bones. It was just another foggy, dreary, dark, and melancholic day, typical for this time of the year. The wind caused soft rustling of leaves, and the temperature was dropping by the hour. I briefly looked at the leaves shaking on the trees outside. The brilliant reds, golds, oranges, and yellows were variegated shades that only Mother Nature could have produced. Every now and then, one of them would break apart dance with the wind then vanish into the evening sky. Soon, the trees would be stripped bare, and winter would be here.

Mother Nature! I thought about that for a moment. "Mother" Nature? . I shook my head . This was the creative work of our Lord. I know that Almighty God, Elohim, the Creator of this universe; took His own time and created these luscious trees of green that give us all these beautiful colors like clockwork every single year. I whispered, "Lord, I thank you for the eyes you have blessed me with to see your beautiful creations. Now you might ask where this came from? Well, it came as a result of the various lessons I learned in my life.

What are these extraordinary lifetime lessons? Well I have had many. Mama used to say, "A bought lesson is a learned lesson." I do not think I fully understood the significance of those words of wisdom when I first heard them. However, over time, I developed an appreciation for them. Contemplating my life experiences, I can honestly say that I know, that I know, that I know the validity of the lessons I have learned. I bought every one of them throughout my life. They have stood the test of time. Therefore, I will not tell you what I heard or what might be; or even what somebody told me. Instead, I will tell you what I *know* for a fact.

I know because I paid a royal price for these lessons. That price includes my health, my emotions, my joy, and my security. I am usually thankful that it did not cost me my life; although it did alter the quality of my life in such a way that I am not always feeling as thankful or optimistic as I should. As I laid my head back on the pillow and gazed up at the painting, I thought back to another time, a time when my big heart proved to be greater than all the theories and principles of teaching with which I had armed myself in preparation for the teaching profession.

I was trained by the best and was excited about the profession I had chosen. I thought it would all be easy. I would teach the children to speak correctly, and they would be excited about leaving their classmates for some one-on-one or small-group therapy with me. We would play games, and I would reward them with treats. It all seemed straightforward to me. For example, I would teach little "Wyo'nee Miff" to correctly pronounce his name, Rodney Smith. Unfortunately, it did not work the way I had anticipated and planned for it. I cried. I literally shed tears because one of the little ones whom I taught was not as excited about speech therapy as I was. You guessed it; I was living in the land of "They lived happily ever after." I lived in fairy-tale land, completely detached from the cold harshness of reality.

⚜

I excitedly began my career as a speech pathologist. My first job was in a poor South Carolina county that was over a thousand miles east of the city in Texas where I was presented those paintings.

I audibly groaned as I forced myself back to the present. As I turned over in the opposite direction, my eyes found my high school graduation picture on the wall across the room. As memories began flooding my mind again, I reached to open the top drawer on the bedside table. I pulled out my high school yearbook and began flipping through its pages. *I was so young,* I thought. So young, so trusting, so naïve, so optimistic, so full of life and energy. I had such high expectations for my life. I genuinely believed that if I worked hard and followed the Golden Rule of treating people the way I wanted to be treated, I would have a successful life. Of course, by now, I learned that this was not necessarily the case.

With my yearbook in hand, I reminded myself that there was much in it for me to be proud of. First, I was educated in a historic Rosenwald School. It was during the Jim Crow-separate but equal era. We had gifted teachers who made learning challenging as they prepared us to compete in the unjust society we faced. I reflected briefly on my years at ole Rosenwald, where I attended grades 1 through 12. I opened my yearbook and slowly turned the pages to the senior superlatives. I was voted most likely to succeed in life. That made me smile. Eventually, I made it to the page dedicated to the school's basketball team; I played varsity basketball in high school. I smiled, recalling how I had not made the team the first two years when I tried out. I was too large to fit in the uniforms that were available for our high school team. Our team received hand-me-down uniforms whenever the district purchased new ones for the white schools. Although I was not the best of players, I felt better telling myself that I was not chosen because none of the uniforms fit me. Fortunately, I did manage to make the team during my junior year, and it was at that time that our school purchased new uniforms. That was a huge deal for us. I was personally measured to ensure that one fit my chubby body.

However, even after I made the team, I was still not a great player. But practice makes perfect, and over time, I climbed my way up the ranks. By twelfth grade, I had improved my skills enough to start as the forward on our championship team. I am thankful that the girls' team still played half-court! At the same time, I was also a member of the high school band. I flipped through the yearbook to find my band's picture. I thought I was cool to be on it when I was in school, but looking back on it now, I smiled as I remembered how pitiful, utterly pitiful, we actually were. We had great drummers and majorettes. We knew how to step to the rhythm. Our claim to fame was our rhythmic high-stepping march.

We wore wool, royal-blue, and gold hand-me-down uniforms in band. We received them when the white school bought new uniforms for its marching band. They were very generous because as horrible as we sounded, they would have been within their rights to deny us uniforms. That thought made me laugh.

Moreover, I was also president of a few school clubs. The student body chose me as their homecoming queen. I was crowned Miss Rosenwald during the halftime performance at the homecoming game. I was unanimously chosen by the school body to represent the school. That was a proud time for my mother and me. My mother and I walked all over town to find that perfect royal-blue suit. I even sewed a fur collar on the wool suit we found; I was quite a seamstress. I looked good, I was sharp as a tack, and my parents were proud of me! Reminiscing about these times—the good times—had me feeling bittersweet. I was happy because of the great time I had but also upset because I did not have it anymore.

꧁ ꧂

Now I had to pull myself out of my past and back to reality. Reality? What is reality? I put the yearbook aside and let my mind continue to travel down memory lane. I decided that I would face those demons no matter how hard it was because regardless of what I might relive, I would at last be able to face up to what caused me to become paralyzed.

Why now? I wondered. *Why this sudden sense of urgency to write my story after waiting for so many years? Why now of all times?* After a lot of introspection, I came up with two reasons justifying why there was no better time than now to write this story. One, I had just celebrated my seventieth birthday. I am emotionally sound for the present, but I do not know what tomorrow holds. Better to fulfill this duty before it was too late than never to get started in the first place. Second, I had become a victim of domestic abuse again! Before it was a boyfriend. This time it was my husband.

During a group counseling session, I learned that I share common personality traits that attract abusers. God, without a doubt, does everything for good, just as Romans 8:28 proclaims. Somehow, certain emotional needs of mine were not met during my childhood, and I consequently share traits with people who also try to resolve their emotional issues through relationships. We all care too deeply for people. We put their needs before our own. We want to help them to a degree where we deny ourselves. As a result, we end up repeating the same vicious cycle in our relationships that we dealt with in our pasts. That opens us up to be abused and being mistreated.

If we take inventory of ourselves, we find that we are abused by family members, friends, and even by colleagues on the job. This disorder is described in the book *Women Who Love Too Much* by Robin Norwood. I am only now learning to love myself and accept that God made me in His image. I do not need anyone else's approval to live my truth. I am finally learning to trust myself and not worry about pleasing other people who, frankly, have no right to dictate my actions. For the first time in my life, I am learning to take care of myself and my needs without feeling guilty or apologetic. Now that is the freedom Jesus died for—to set me free. Indeed, to set us all free. I confess that it is a hard lesson to learn as there is also a lot of *unlearning* involved. I am still a work in progress. Habits are hard to break, and I was unfortunately raised from the start to be a people pleaser. "What will the people think?" was often said to me. Oh yes, and, "What goes on in this house, stays in this house," was another one. I am learning that we are no sicker than our secrets, so I guess I am still buying that lesson.

Right now, I am trying to completely reprogram my mind. I am learning not to let others define me. I must constantly remind myself that I am made in the image of God and that God loves me exactly as I am. I must live my life the way God intended me to do, and anything less would be dishonorable to His creation. I must love myself. Moreover, I try to praise God for the strength and peace He affords me through the tragedies of my life. No matter how it hurts, I know that God is working it all together for my good. It does not always come easy, yet I try because I know God's Word is right.

For the first time in as long as I can remember, I can look at my experiences objectively and record them based on facts as I recall them, not as the feelings of a person who was hunted down, chased, trapped, and fired on like a wild animal. I had to put myself in check because despite all the personal abuse I experienced over the years gone by, and the promises I made to myself once I pulled myself out of it, I ended up in another abusive relationship. Or rather, as a member of my counseling group described it, an abusive "situation." Knowing all that I know now, I am fully cognizant of the fact that someone out there needs and will benefit from the lessons God taught me through my struggles. The wise prefer to learn from history, especially when it is readily available for them. Please understand this is not about religion. It was the religious people, the scribes and Pharisees, who killed Jesus. Rather, my story is about a relationship with God through faith in my Lord and Savior, Jesus Christ of Nazareth.

4

ACQUIRING TOUGH
LESSONS

A man is great not because he hasn't failed; a man
is great because failure hasn't stopped him.

CONFUCIUS

A glance at my early childhood and teenage years would make anyone think I was a brilliant student, destined to rise to the pinnacle of excellence. In fact, I was voted Most Likely to Succeed in the 1967 yearbook of my small-town high school. Despite being in the segregated South, my fellow schoolmates were confident I would be able to rise above all adversities and make something of myself. For my part, I was fully on course to fulfill my schoolmates' prophesy.

I worked hard through college and managed to graduate a semester earlier. Soon after, I landed my first job as a public-school speech pathologist at the young age of twenty. At the time, I was still dating my high school and college sweetheart. We were planning to get married and have five children together. Why five children? Well we were enrolled in the same college, where he was one of their best sportsmen. I was a freshman, and we found mutual amusement in the fad of using a simple pendulum to determine the number of children we as a couple should have—but after marriage, of course!

Borrowed from a science classroom project, a group of couples huddled together over a cafeteria table to see what their fortunes were. Someone held a pencil suspended from a string over my wrist. Holding it with a steady hand, the person began swinging it back and forth. My boyfriend counted each complete swing of the pencil as one child. Altogether, we had five consistent swings representing the five children destined in our future. We were young back then and found this activity quite entertaining.

In all honesty, it was all just clean, wholesome fun. It was just something to pass the time. Personally, I thought it was a funny kind of prophesy; after all, five children is quite a lot. Nonetheless, we were two small-town black teenagers with enchanting plans for a successful future. Using our degrees, we planned to land professional jobs with promising careers ahead of us. Since my dad was a builder, we planned to build a fabulous house for ourselves using his help. We intended for the house to be massive, perfect for a happy, prosperous family of seven. During our lengthy discussions, we often talked about what we would name our children or what our house's furnishings would be like. Our future looked great. However, despite everyone's expectations, something went tragically wrong.

In February 1968, during my freshman year at the state college, our students were attempting to integrate the local bowling alley. Remember that this was at the height of the civil rights movement, so this was unprecedented but not uncommon at the time. Initially, about two hundred students staged a nonviolent demonstration at the small bowling alley. We were swiftly dispersed by the local police. However, the issue did not die down.

A few days later, on February 8, 1968, a large group of male students protested on the campus hill, and state troopers were called in. They were supposed to protect our students, but instead, they fired on a group of the young student protesters. Three students were killed and twenty-eight injured in what was thereafter known as the Orangeburg Massacre.

My boyfriend was present on that awful night and witnessed the tragedy firsthand. When they started firing into the crowd, he, like others, had to flee for his life. Around that time, he also suffered the death of his father and brother. After going through all that trauma, he was simply not the same person.

He started drinking excessively and became increasingly demanding and violent. Whenever he became depressed, he took it out on me in the form of arguments and aggressive statements. In retrospect, I wonder if he was suffering from PTSD. Going through so much violence and death in such a short span of time is bound to leave an imprint on anyone's mind. Alas, there I go again, feeling sympathy for the wrong person. I am still a work in progress.

As time progressed, his erratic behavior escalated exponentially. Our fights and arguments became more frequent over time. All of this came to a head one day when, without me doing anything to provoke him, he punched me. The sudden blow threw me to the floor, leaving me too shocked to respond. After flashing an angry glare at me, he calmly walked away, as if punching me was all he needed at that moment. Punching me with his hard fists became a frequent incident between us.

Of course, he was genuinely sorry each time. He always scurried back to me later and apologized profusely, begging me to forgive him. Unfortunately, I, in all my naivety, forgave him every time. But despite however many times he punched me, and I forgave him, it did not do anything to stop the blood from coming out of my nose. It was like I was stuck in some vicious cycle in which I was the victim of his abuse, yet I accepted his apology every time.

Eventually, the abuse became so toxic that it started affecting my academic life. This started one night when he paged me at my dormitory over the intercom system after I told him I had an important assignment to work on and did not have the time to see him for a while. I barely had any time left to work on the assignment, so I decided to continue working, ignoring his attempts to contact me. When I refused to respond to his page, he was enraged. He went into the men's dormitory's kitchen and grabbed a jar of mayonnaise. Then he snuck out and trudged across the campus grounds to the women's dormitories. He walked around the building to the base of my second-floor room's window and then threw the jar through it. The sound of the heavy jar of mayonnaise shattering on my bedroom floor frightened me. I scurried away to sit on the toilet and calm my nerves. Eventually, I emerged and continued my work on the assignment. He did not call me again, but for the rest of the night and many other nights thereafter, I remained on edge.

Despite all the abuse I was subjected to at his hand, I do not recall any other violence directed toward me while we were on campus. It usually happened when we were at home on the weekends or during breaks, away from the eyes of wider society. The fact that he abused me in private made it easier for me to accept it and forgive him. Had there been someone else who saw him hitting me and intervened on my behalf, I might have sooner recognized his violence for what it was.

Despite all that I was suffering through in my private life, I managed to graduate from college a semester earlier than projected. The place where I began working as a public-school speech pathologist was in a town two hours away from my home. I moved to that town a year before the first apartment complex was built, so I secured room and board from an elderly family. Despite the distance, we continued to date, making time for each other wherever we could.

By the time summer rolled around, he wanted us to get married. I, on the other hand, had different feelings. I no longer thought of him as the childhood friend with whom I shared time in the library, reading books, and discussing biology projects. I no longer saw him as a trusted confidant that I could confide in without fear. He was no longer the friend whom I grew up with and planned to marry after college. He was hurting me physically and mentally. He behaved more like an enemy than a friend, let alone a partner. I was young, yet I knew that love was not supposed to hurt. I declined his marriage proposal by simply saying that I was not ready for marriage quite yet. I could not tell him the truth. I could not tell him that my love and respect for him had diminished with each violent attack. I wanted to ease out of the relationship. However, I was scared that if I revealed any of this to him, he would retaliate violently. So, for the moment, I decided to give him a soft rejection that would not hurt his ego.

He did not take being refused very well and tried everything to convince me to marry him. He bought an engagement ring and coerced me into wearing it. To protect myself, I wore it when I knew I had to be in his company, but since I did not want to have to explain it to everyone else, I kept it off for the most part. He even resorted to peer pressure by telling all of our friends that we were engaged. He knew how private I was and that I would not tell any of my friends about the abuse. Nor would I try correcting his lies.

Finally, I recognized that things were getting out of hand and that I needed advice. I sought counsel from one of our best friends, who I knew would give it to me straight. Moreover, I knew that he had both of our well-beings at heart. He told me that the decision had to be mine and mine alone. However, whatever I decided in the end, I had to stick to it. I thought carefully about what it was that I really wanted, and once I was sure, I told our friend that I wanted to end the relationship forever.

I was going to get my daddy to talk to my "boyfriend" and explain to him that he must leave me alone. It was clear to me that he would not listen to whatever I had to say. I thought that it would be better if my father were the one who told him. I was sure he would respect his authority. Our friend told me that I needed to be sure about what I wanted before involving my dad because once I told my dad, I would not be good to change my mind. I nodded, assuring him that I was confident about not wanting to be in a relationship with him any longer. At this, our friend reiterated what he had said earlier, "After you involve your daddy, you must not change your mind. You must be sure." I did not understand why he was cautioning me repeatedly. I was sure. Who would not be? I was tired of constantly being beaten.

I was fearful of my "boyfriend" and wanted out of the relationship. I could not wait any longer. I had to tell my daddy that his beloved daughter was being abused and needed his help.I mustered up the strength to talk to my dad in the most positive manner possible. (*as if there is a positive way to tell a man that his precious little girl is being assaulted by the very person who should love and protect her.*) My level-headed daddy listened quietly, then assured me that he would tell him that he was no longer welcome to our home, and he should comply with my decision to no longer date him.

My gentle daddy politely explained to my "boyfriend" that I did not want to date him or associate with him in any shape or form. Furthermore, Dad told him that he was no longer welcome to visit our house, something he had the right to do since we were children. He was to leave me alone and be on his way.

I had hoped that coming from my dad, one of the male authority figures in his life, he would listen and stay away. Unfortunately, those efforts failed. He straight up threatened to harm my family if I did not marry him immediately. Since I now refused to meet with him and it was clear I wanted nothing to do with him, he began stalking me. I became increasingly paranoid whenever I was out of my house and was always on the lookout for him.

I welcomed the return of the new school year as it took me away from my hometown, where he lived. I moved into an apartment and was assigned to a school in a town twenty-five miles away from my previous school building. At last, I was at peace and did not have to be fearful of my abuser. Unfortunately, this breath of relief did not last awfully long. I was terrified when I found out he had managed to track my new workplace down through a former employer. I was stunned when he walked right into my classroom minutes before school ended.

When I looked at the intruder walking into my room, what I noticed first were alcohol-induced red eyes and a dark purple shirt. I was in my classroom alone, yet I had no time to consider how embarrassed I was because of how sudden it all was. After glaring at me for a while, he stepped out of the room. I did not know where he had gone, so the moment the bell rang, I rushed out. Normally I stayed back awhile to prepare for the next day, but not that day. I headed straight for the parking lot and got into the car.

As I turned the ignition, I heard another car next to mine come to life as well. I looked to my right and saw him in his car, glaring at me. I immediately pulled out and turned onto the highway. Now that we were in our cars, he began chasing me, driving aggressively behind me on the twenty-five-mile highway stretch to my meeting spot at the district office in the town where I shared an apartment with two other speech pathologists.

Now that he knew where I worked, I also did not want him to know where I lived. Nor did I want to lead him to the district office lest he also disrupt my meeting there. So instead of leading him to something important, I decided to try and lose him through town. I began taking abrupt turns and swiftly changing lanes to lose him. However, he continued chasing me around the town. I was getting late for my meeting, and by this time, my gas had begun running low, and I was not sure how much gas he had left. So with an exasperated sigh, I gave up and went to my meeting anyway.

As he pulled up beside me in the parking lot, I had to speak with him so I could go to the meeting. He said he wanted to have lunch with me, and I agreed to go with him and discuss everything after my meeting. He said he would wait for me in the parking lot, and I agreed. I went to my meeting, though I could barely concentrate because of how ambivalent I was about our lunch together. After the meeting, we went to a nearby diner. I did not want to eat, so I just sat and talked.

I insisted that our relationship was over and that I could not see him as my boyfriend anymore. At first he was resistant and continued to demand that I marry him. However, I eventually convinced him to back off and leave town. Before leaving, he insisted that I kiss him, so I gave him a quick smack on his puckered lips and reiterated that he must keep his end of the agreement and leave town because I had met and spoken with him as agreed. After he left the diner, I got in my car and went home. On the drive back, I realized that it was important I tell someone about this so that there were witnesses for future reference. I told my coworkers about it, who were also my roommates, after I returned from lunch with him. I had been too embarrassed to tell them about him waiting outside the meeting. Despite how nerve-wracking the entire ordeal had been, I thought this was the last of it. I had managed to sever my ties with him finally. Or so I thought.

However, something in the back of my mind kept insisting that I was still in danger and needed to take precautions. Therefore, while visiting my parents' home the next weekend, I contacted our hometown police officer to ask for advice. He recommended that I get a gun to protect myself. I was aghast at the suggestion. I was terrified of guns. I would never get one for myself! Besides, I would never have the heart to use it against anyone, including my abusive, stalker ex-boyfriend. My own common sense also alerted me to the fact that a gun would only add to my troubles rather than alleviate them. A gun just did not seem like a solution. It would look like a shootout between two black adults if I were to get one, knowing what my ex's temperament was like. Besides, even if we survived that shootout, we would both just end up in jail. That was not going to be me! I would never use a gun. Never! A gun was simply out of the question.

Whenever I was home over the weekends, I was afraid to go out because he was always looking for me, wanting to talk. One such weekend, my roommates visited my parents' home with me. We went out that night only to be chased by him. He spotted my car, and the chase began. It only ended when we retreated to my parents' house. The three of us jumped out of the car and ran inside before he could get to me. I must admit he did not come on our property. He did respect some of my father's instructions. Back at work, he had to pass my coworker's school to get to mine. Her workday ended a few minutes before my sessions. She called the school to warn me when she spotted his auto headed to my school. Fortunately, it was my planning period, so I promptly gathered my things and checked out for the day. I was able to avoid him like this for quite some time, except for one time when he chased me in the car until I finally gave up and talked to him. I was able to convince him to go back home. I was careful not to let him know where I lived. He did as he promised, yet I drove to the edge of town and watched him leave town down the highway surrounded with moss-draped trees. Then I went back to my apartment and told my roommates about my ordeal.

I continued to hope that despite being defenseless, I would stay safe. A few months later, I returned home for Thanksgiving. Our social club, which consisted of a group of progressive young professional women, had rented out the local tavern to host a private party. When I returned, I immediately connected with two other party planners, who also happened to be two of my best girlfriends, to ensure that everything was ready. We put the drinks in my parents' freezer so they would be cold in the next hour or two. We then readied the chicken salad. The final task on the checklist was to stop at the tavern to make sure the building was prepared. He was inside the tavern, waiting for me. I spotted him the moment we walked inside as if my eyes were naturally drawn to his furious glare. My girlfriends knew about him, and I quickly alerted them of his presence. They became extremely worried and rushed me to our car.

He dashed after us. We got into the car, but before the driver could speed off, he jumped in through the unlocked door. I got out of the car from the other side before he could do anything drastic and ran out into the yard. He got out of the car and ran after me. He managed to make up the distance between us and caught me by my left arm. That was when he pulled a gun from the waist of his pants.

I was momentarily confused. When he pointed the weapon at me, I pleaded with him to spare my life, "No, Nory, no!" It was in vain.

On that night, my ex-boyfriend, who supposedly loved me to death, shot me three times in the head, all while holding my hand. I died and felt my spirit leave my body. I remember the sensation well. Time seemed to slow to a still as his finger pulled the trigger.

Pow!

I felt the bullet clip my head with a thump near my ear. Then a high-frequency noise rang throughout my head. Instinctively, I threw up my right arm to protect my face.

Pow!

My arm did little to protect me. The bullet traveled through the flesh of my arm and struck me in my right forehead.

Pow!

Another bullet hit me directly in the head. I fell to the cold ground. Time had ground to a stop in my head, so I felt like I was falling in slow motion. As my body hit the ground, it felt as if my body bounced up and down. Yes, I felt like I kept falling over and over in slow motion. In my final moments, I remembered deciding to give up, to just stop struggling. Our friend was shot in the shoulder as he attempted to stop him from killing me. He fell to the ground, groaning in pain.

I am told my ex kicked me violently as I lay on the ground, face down in a puddle of water. Someone eventually convinced him to stop, but he just put the gun to his own head and shot himself. However, the bullet only managed to scrape the surface of his forehead. With that, he just gave up and went home in a daze, where he told his mother that someone shot him. Poor lady. I was told that once he left, someone moved my face out of the puddle to prevent me from drowning.

Yet despite how horrific this violent incident was, I came back. God honored the pleas and petitions of my family as well as the prayers of a community that was in shock over its occurrence. One of my parents' friends later confided in me as she talked of the night I was critically wounded. "Even I prayed for you," she said, "and I don't pray." I was shocked because I thought everybody that age prayed. My suffering not only brought the whole community together but also brought some closer to God.

I was quickly taken to the hospital, where the doctors immediately began treating me. I was told that their attempts to revive me were hard-fought but pessimistic. They had no expectations for me to have a productive life if I recovered. *If* I recovered at all. Despite this, I survived and defied all their predictions. Yes, God answered all those prayers. I was alive, well, and mostly mobile. I was paralyzed but happy to be alive. I was determined to continue my life. This incident was not going to hamper me from achieving what I had been working so hard to achieve. My classmates thought that I was most likely to succeed. They spoke it, and I had to fulfill it!

Despite the paralysis, I worked twenty-two years as a teacher. Although I faced ignorance and prejudice because of these special conditions, I persevered. I raised my daughter alone, which was a struggle I am proud of. Marriage to her father was brief and problematic. The divorce was fretful, but faith in God was, once again, my foundation for survival. I was involved with churches that had strong teaching ministries. I joined a great home-based Bible study that taught me about the faithfulness of God as well as the power of prayer. I also took advantage of written, audiotapes, and televised ministries. By the grace of God, I worked hard and provided a great living for myself and my precious little daughter.

By the time I was forty-five years old, I suffered from overuse syndrome in my right hand and arm. I was an ordained pastor who was medically retired while preparing for certification as a mental health chaplain. During the tenure of my ministry, I faced even greater ignorance and prejudice, reaching levels that were dangerous. I experienced firsthand that the "Church will kill its wounded." That experience proved to be a greater hindrance to my recovery than all others. While my faith was not in humankind, the ministry opened my eyes to the fact that religion can sometimes fail. It was around this time I bought the lesson that people can fail, but sound teaching can produce an unrelenting faith in God through a personal relationship with Jesus Christ. After all that I have been through, I have developed into a woman of great faith. I have experienced great victories and enjoyed fellowship with God. However, all that did not prevent my next heartache, my next quandary.

At the age of sixty-two, I met and married my soul mate. Yes, I met him on the internet. It was a Christian dating site. Indeed, I was cautious. I did a pretty thorough background check, and he checked out. We seemed to have a lot in common. He was a Christian and enjoyed worshipping at nondenominational churches. Many refer to them as "Word churches" because of the great emphasis on teaching God's Word. He had some physical ailments consequential to combat in the Vietnam war. He appeared to love me and was accepting of my physical limitations.

I met his wonderful mother on the short visit to his hometown. He drove by his efficiency apartment, pointed to it, and said, "That is where I live." I was surprised but without judgment of his meager living quarters. I understood he lost everything during the process of applying for Social Security disability after he suffered a stroke. I empathized with him because I, too, had to live more than six months without an income during the process of determining Social Security eligibility. I survived the process because I had insurance that covered my mortgage during the process. It was indeed a difficult time. I understood how emotionally and economically devastating it is when illness prevents one from working. I discerned that there were benefits that he could receive from his veteran's connection and promised to help him get them. This would help both of us. In the meantime, he moved to my home and helped out with the bills until he could contribute more. After all, marriage is about sharing, helping, supporting, and compromise. That was the model I witnessed from my parents. It worked extremely well for them, and I wanted to have a marriage like theirs. I believed that God had finally sent me a companion of equal mind and faith to grow old with. I could finally exhale. God answered my prayers for a great marriage like my parents, who at the time had been married sixty-three successful years!

The first year we did well. We traveled and were able to enjoy the social benefits of being a couple. Eventually, there were struggles at home that increased with time. In the process of applying for his veteran's disability, he was enrolled in therapy at the veteran's hospital that forced him to recall details of the war experience that he suppressed for more than forty years. His experience in Vietnam was so devastating that he hallucinated on rainy days. He said when it rained, he could see the tracers and hear the bullets. It caused paralyzing fear. He had soaking night sweats almost every night. He talked about his near-death experiences but refused to talk about parts of the war that were too grievous to detail. It was too upsetting to list them on his application for disability, yet therapy forced him to relive the sordid details that he tried so hard to forget. Around the same time, he experienced the death of a significant family member. He changed. He started drinking and throwing the beer cans on my beautiful carpeted floor. When I complained, he insisted that I was wrong. I did a lot of self-examination and concluded that I had a right to protect my assets.

He became controlling and unwilling to share my own property with me. He quickly played the role of the victim when I asserted my rights. I admitted that I had issues and baggage yet, but I was not wrong for insisting on being treated with respect. I had a right to enjoy some of the fruits of my years of work. I did not mind sharing, but I was *not* going to deny myself the use of things I bought. I concluded that my husband was not as emotionally stable as I had initially made him out to be.

Then I was diagnosed with non-Hodgkin's lymphoma, a cancer of the lymphatic system. Things went horribly wrong for me once again. By that time, my new husband, who is a year older than me, began drinking excessively. He became cold and distant. He told me that he knew I was going to die before him. I was too flabbergasted to respond. I realized that he was shutting me out. He would go out to eat without inviting me. I tolerated his behavior with the excuse that I didn't like to eat the unhealthy foods he ate. When it was my treat, he ordered the most expensive item on the menu. He even started going to church alone. I prayed and yes, I did complain. He was soft-spoken except for a few bursts of anger. The use of profanity was common to him. I grew to understand that it was a part of his life. My family did not use profanity and taught me that it was unacceptable, but I tolerated it because that was who he was.

I was encouraged when he offered that we go to marriage counseling at the VA hospital. I wondered briefly why he smirked as he invited me to come to therapy with him. Eventually, I realized that he—honestly, I don't to this day understand why he drove us to therapy and then just sat there without participating. On occasions, he used that time as opportunities to criticize me. The chemotherapy caused me to be emotional, so I cried a lot as I worked to meet the objectives of therapy. My husband was cold and obstinate as he refused to do any assignments. On the last day we attended therapy, he walked out shortly after the start of the session but waited for me downstairs. I was ambivalent about the ride home with him; therefore, I prearranged a ride with a friend. When he left the therapy session, he went out quietly and without incident, but our therapist gave me the telephone number to Sister Care and emphatically suggested that I contact them.

I was vaguely aware of Sister Care. I knew it was an organization that helped people experiencing domestic violence. My husband was not hitting me, so I did not understand why I needed Sister Care. I took a quick inventory of our relationship. He was emotionally absent and refused to equally contribute to the household budget. He was building his savings account at my expense. That is the epitome of selfishness, but I didn't think that was abuse. So I filed the phone number for Sister Care in my jacket pocket and forgot it. It was December. I wanted to have a good Christmas, so I decided to forget it. I admit that I was giving, and he was taking while blaming me for making him feel unwelcome in my house. Still, I did not see how that was abuse.

Feeling conflicted, I prayed and trusted God for help and protection as I could not bear the idea of yet another failed marriage. I prayed and stayed with my husband, hoping things would improve. God heard my prayer and kept the promise He made in 1 Corinthians 10:13 (KJV): "There hath no temptation taken you but such as is common to man: but God is faithful, who will not suffer you to be tempted above that ye are able; but will with the temptation also make a way to escape, that ye may be able to bear it."

A month or two later, I was surfing the internet and came across a house in our community for sale. It was larger than the one we lived in. Although I am not a lawyer, I do know enough about the law to know that women before me who invited their husbands into their homes had trouble removing the husband from the premise when things got volatile. Just on a whim, I asked my husband to go with me to see the property. He refused, but after my pleas, he reluctantly went. I loved the house, and the price was right. He was not interested. I painted the perfect picture. He would use his VA certificate to get the no money down option, and we could buy this house. He could park his desired boat on the right. The picture I painted of the boat he dreamed of owning was enough for him to give me the okay to start the process. What I did not know was that my husband was hiding his money from me. By now he was receiving his VA disability benefits but used them to build his savings. He would not supply any of his financial records to help us qualify for the house. I was perplexed. But the mortgage company said I had enough personal credit and savings to satisfy the loan process. I went forth with the process, and we got the loan.

I sold my used furniture and used my savings to purchase all new furniture for the new house. He leased the moving van to move the major things on the first day. After that day, he moved his personal belongings but refused to help me. I had to get help to complete the move. I finally got everything moved, and the new furniture was starting to be delivered. I heard him tell his son that it was *his* house, not *our* house. I angrily corrected him by reminding him that I had to put up the financing to qualify for the mortgage. A few days later, he announced that he would make the mortgage payments. I must admit that I experienced a momentary sigh of relief, until reality forced me to deduce that he might try to force me out of the house because I had another house a few blocks away.

In April, four months after our last marriage counseling session, a male and female police officer responded to my call for help at our newly acquired residence. The male officer accosted my husband in the yard as he attempted to hide outside the house. Without incident, he surrendered the reported weapon, a gigantic hunting knife. He was visibly intoxicated as he incriminated himself by attempting to justify his actions. He confessed, claiming he was protecting himself. In the meantime, the female officer was inside with me. She listened to my side of what happened. After talking to her partner, who remained outside with my husband, she told me to leave the house and suggested that I contact Sister Care, a nonprofit organization that provides services and advocacy for survivors of domestic violence. I grabbed my jacket. I put my hand in the pocket, and the phone number that the marriage counselor gave me in December was there. I had not worn that jacket since that December day. At last I understood why the VA counselor gave me the phone number to Sister Care. Finally, I connected the dots.

The marriage counselor recognized that I was experiencing abuse. I guess that her obligation was to the veteran and, therefore, could not counsel me, yet she recommends that I get help. I vowed that I would not tolerate any form of abuse. But I did tolerate abuse because I did not perceive that abuse is a monster with many disguises.

God physically delivered me out of this abusive marriage before I was physically hurt. Before I married my husband, I told him of my previous experience with domestic violence and let him know that I would not tolerate any abuse. Once I recognized my plight as abuse,

I took legal steps to protect myself until I was legally divorced. While going through that experience, I was horrified to find that after fifty years, the advice from the police was the same. A day later I went to the police department to follow up on the incident, find out my rights, and their suggested recourse. I had a house full of belongings that I wanted. I was afraid because I did not know what he might do. The police advised me to get a gun.

A different officer made the following statement to me as he escorted me to our house a week later to pick up my much-needed personal belongings: "My wife won't let me abuse her." Was he saying that because of my physical limitations? Was he saying that I allowed my husband to abuse me? I did not respond. I just thought, *how incompetent is the police force! How chauvinistic is that policeman!* I wondered why, after so many deaths due of domestic violence, someone had not figured out that officers need training. I realize you cannot teach compassion or common sense. I also question if the laws are weak because many people in power abuse their spouses and believe that it is right.

That experience taught me that after all these years, the police still did not have a clue. My husband was abusive. Yet the police told me that I had to leave our house, in which I was the major investor and owned everything in the house. It did not matter that I am a woman, that it was at night, or that I had to find somewhere to live because my husband was drunk and abusive. He was allowed to stay in the house. He caused the problem, yet I was ordered to leave with nothing but the clothes on my back. Why assume that the husband is the owner of everything? Times have changed.

One day, after the embarrassment of having the police escort me to my house to get my belongings, I spoke to my new neighbor. Out of frustration, I told the stranger why I had to have the police escort me to my house. She advised me to get a lawyer because he could sue me for abandonment. I did not have the money, but I did get an attorney.

When we appeared in court, he quickly said, "She abandoned

the home and refused to return." I thank God for leading me to that neighbor. Because of her, I found the money to get an attorney, who was able to show that I left him legally with an order of protection and set the process in place to get a divorce. I just wanted my things out of the house. Within the year, I got the divorce. The judge ordered that we sell the house. I got financing and purchased the house. By and by, I got back everything that I lost plus some. (Twenty years earlier, I was stressing over my situation and pleaded to God for change. God told me to read the book of Job. When I did not understand, He told me to read the end.)

I must admit it was stressful, the process hurt, and it was expensive. But God provided. No, I did not borrow any money from family or friends. Pride did not allow me to tell anyone how distressful the situation was. For the first time in my life, I took advantage of credit cards to pay the attorney. I learned some valuable lessons on when to use credit instead of cash. My attorney helped my husband get back his VA certificate. I had to pay the down payment to buy the house. It was an impossible situation, but God provided. I had to make so many choices. I now had two mortgages. How was I going to manage it all? But God! Yes, I prayed, and as always, God guided. God provided. He showed me what to do. I ran into a snag or two, but I made it.

I wondered if I overreacted. Should I have given my husband another chance? I was angry about my situation. I was fearful, and I was depressed. His mother and siblings were the best parts of my marriage. I mourned the loss. I thank God for the experience. I bought that expensive lesson, but thanks to God's guidance in management and to Sister Care, there was a safe place for counseling and emotional support. It took work. It takes work. It will forever take work. Time heals all pains.

I sought counseling to understand how I repeated this cycle of attraction to abusive and emotionally unavailable men. Thanks to this counseling, I learned that there was nothing wrong with me. I did not fail God, nor did I make another "stupid" mistake. This new predicament I found myself in caused me to pray more and develop the necessary tools to become a more confident person. The lesson I learned during this painful experience was that I need to set boundaries. I need to ask myself, "What is in it for me?" Yes, I need to learn to be a bit more selfish. I am a helper at heart, and unfortunately, there are people who live to take advantage of that. Yes, people do mistake kindness for weakness. It was about time I bought this expensive lesson. I smile because as frustrating and stressful as it was, deep down in my soul, I knew that God Himself had promised to work this together for my good (Romans 8: 28). I remind myself to praise God because I have victory in Christ Jesus. Looking back, I am stronger because of that experience.

Let me explain further. God is no respecter of persons. I am not pious. Any presumptions that God will side with me because I am me are exactly that, presumptions. I learned the lesson that God loves us all. I must stand before God with a clear conscious that I did all that was in my power to follow peace, even when peace was not offered to me. I am not claiming to be perfect, not by a long shot. But I know my response was pleasing and acceptable to God. Therefore, I stand on God's promises in Isaiah 54:17 (KJV): No weapon that is formed against thee shall prosper." I wholeheartedly bought the lesson that two wrongs do not make a right, which is why Jesus taught in Matthew 5:44 (KJV), "But I say unto you, Love your enemies, bless them that curse you, do good to them that hate you, and pray for them which despitefully use you, and persecute you."

Love is universal; it cannot be selective. I cannot choose whom I love and whom I do not because in that case, even those I naively choose to love will only be loved spitefully. I must love everyone as everyone is God's handcrafted creations. Now that does not mean I need to stay in harm's way. You never know what tragedy might unfold. If there is any threat of danger, follow your intuition, and secure your personal safety. Wisely and carefully make your exit. Once you know the voice of God, He will guide you. In other words, know when it is time to leave.

You might ask, "How does one know when it is time to leave?" Life has taught me that it is better to be safe than sorry. Sorry is a sorry word. My abuser, the person who shot me and rendered me paralyzed for life, was sorry. I understand that he cried whenever he saw how much he damaged my life. Indeed, he was anguished and repentant, but that does not take away the pain that I feel today as I hurt from my neck to my waist on the left side of my body. And my arm and fingers on the right side swell and hurt as I pen this book. When my right arm hurts, my life stops. I cannot drive or do my daily living tasks. I have no hands to use. Those are the times I hold onto God's hand, and He carries me through the wave of depression. Better days do come.

The person who murdered his spouse is sorry, but that does not change the fact it happened and cannot be reversed. No, I am not angry; God helped me to forgive. I had to in order to survive. Am I glad I did! I cannot change the past, but I pray that through sharing my experiences, I can help somebody avoid impending doom.

Experience has taught me that abuse is a monster with many disguises. I acquired these lessons through personal experience. I will briefly list a few disguises of that monster.

1. The abuser is cunning: He or she can be loving and gentle. After a violent blow, be it verbal or physical, the abuser is genuinely sorry and promises never to do it again. After a while, the abuser blames the victim by asserting that he or she caused the abuser to react violently and, therefore, deserved the outcome. "See what you made me do?" he says so convincingly. This is a subtle form of brainwashing.

2. The abuser is indoctrinating: He or she convinces the victim to accept a set of false beliefs. "No one will believe you." "You cannot leave me because no one else will want you." "You are not smart enough." "You are fat and or ugly." "You need me to survive." This is a blatant form of brainwashing.

3. The abuser uses humiliation: The victim is forced to secrecy for fear of shame, guilt, or to protect a personal or business reputation. The victim attempts to protect the reputations of the family in the community. "The Bible says you must submit to me. You don't want people to know you are ruining our marriage. What will your family say?"

4. Threats against children or family members: The victim compelled to protect family. The abuser manipulates the victim by threatening to harm loved ones. Attack on family members hurts the victim.

5. Financial withholdings: When one partner controls the money and gains power and control by limiting the victim's resources, he or she is trapped with no way out.

6. Isolation from friends and family. The abuser will seek to take away friends and family. The victim will be helpless with no one to turn to, therefore, he or she must remain with the abuser.

7. Fear and intimidation: The abuser exhibit a range of unpredictable temperaments that keep the victim fearful and ill at ease. The victim might appear unstable to an onlooker, thus making the abuser appear to be the healthy, stable person in the relationship. Many victims appear to be the aggressor and end up in jail, especially when they fight back.

8. Physical abuse. The abuser at this point has no self-control nor fear of going to jail. Abuse can be deadly either by intent or by accident. When it gets physical, it is dangerous. If the victim fights back, he or she may end up in jail. If not to do so might bring death or injury. Again, know when it is time to leave.

9. Adultery: When a spouse dishonors the marriage vows, it causes emotional abuse to the person being cheated on. Adultery is such a severe sin that God included it in the Ten Commandments: "Thou shall not commit adultery (Exodus 20:14 KJV). Adultery hurts the entire family.

10. Obscure and ambiguous: Because abuse has so many disguises, it can be difficult to recognize. Even after that abuser is identified, the victim, due to emotional attachment or habit, may protect him or her or be in denial of the imminent danger. The victim is often trapped and confused. The children suffer.

11. Delusions: The victim may develop an altered reality. He or she often makes excuses for the abuser's bad behavior or convinces himself or herself that it is not happening. Victims can believe deadly abuse never happens to them or their loved ones, so they ignore reality.

If you are experiencing any of the above, believe your eyes, believe your reality. Fear that you may become a subject on the local news. It *can* happen to you. I never thought it would happen to me, but it did. I bought these lessons the hard way. I have suffered for it in ways I cannot list. Many have died or caused the death of friends and family members. If any of these abusers are troubling you, get help now. Each state has organizations for domestic violence.

National Coalition Against Domestic Violence (NCADV)
The National Domestic violence hotline is 1 800799SAFE (7233)

Reflections on Acquired Lessons

Society has changed. Morality has suffered. Abuse must end!

At the risk of sounding preachy, I am compelled to make some necessary suggestions on breaking the cycle of abuse.

Based on some personal observations and experiences, abusers often experienced some form of abuse while growing up. They are often children of abusive parents. It is never the victim's fault. When a spouse remains in an abusive relationship, it sends the wrong message to their children and fuels the cycle of abuse to another generation. Know that love does not hurt. Love yourself enough to set boundaries. Love your family enough to get help.

The yo-yo response to abuse is dangerous. Like a yo-yo, you leave then go back repeatedly. That is a setup for disaster.

The lessons I bought have suggested to me ways to break the cycle of abuse. Abuse is indeed a serious matter. Too many people lose their lives or suffer life-altering traumas due to abuse. Yet people seem indifferent; they think that abuse will not happen to them or their loved ones.

Since the beginning of recorded history, women have made false reports of abuse. The Bible, in Genesis 39, offers details of a false report of abuse. Women and men alike make false claims of abuse. Those kinds of false reports make it difficult for law enforcement officers to discern what is true. Please stop that madness as you are hurting people! You are contributing to the culture of abuse.

Teach your children about Jesus. Not about denominations, but a respect for God. And beginning at a young age, provide them with knowledge of the Word of God.

Teach your daughters to get education and training that ensures their financial independence. Teach them that although it is noble be a housewife and rear their children, they need to have their own resources. Every spouse should have his or her own money. It promotes harmony and reduces the roles of absolute power and control. When your girls are young, give them money; teach them to work and be responsible money managers so that a "monster" will not lure them with money.

Teach your sons to get education and training, so they can enjoy financial independence. Prepare them to provide financially for themselves and eventually for their families. Mothers and fathers teach your sons to respect females. Talk to them about the need to be responsible enough to have children when they are ready to be committed fathers.

Pivotal lessons!

5

INSIGHTFUL LESSONS

Face your deficiencies and acknowledge them;
but do not let them master you. Let them teach
you patience, sweetness, and insight.

HELEN KELLER

It is impossible to visit my childhood memories without thinking of visits to my grandmother's house. She was my paternal grandmother and lived about a block from our house. She was 103 years old when she went home to be with the Lord. She entered her eternal rest about nineteen years ago. She loved her grandchildren so much, and we loved her immensely in return. I enjoyed the stories she told me during my visits about as much as I enjoyed the food she always gave me.

"How are you doing, Grandma?" I asked as I hobbled past her, taking special care to maneuver my tripod cane to avoid hitting her feet. I sat in the chair across from her favorite seat in the corner of her bedroom on the other side of the oil stove.

"I'm so glad you came," Grandma said, smiling. "Did you walk all the way up here?"

"Yes, it's only about a block. I'm really okay," I assured her.

"My lass," Grandma said. She sighed loudly as she looked at me. I could almost see the pain in her voice when she said, "When you was a little girl, you had a strong voice." I smiled, thinking she must have recently heard me sing. She must now know that I can no longer carry a tune—even in a bucket with a handle on it. She continued, using colloquial Ebonics. "You sat on that porch out there in a rockin' chair. You was so tiny that yo' legs rested on the seat while you sung in the loud voice of a three- or four-year-old. You had a strong voice. You sung loud and proud, 'There Ain't neee'va gonna be no peace in da valley for me.' You would rock your little body and repeat, 'There ain't neee'va gonna be no peace in da valley for me!'" Grandma held her head down to meet her palm. She ran her fingers roughly through the strands as if to maul her wig off. "You musta knownd what you was talking about." She sighed again. "Umph, umph, uhmmm." With that, an eerie silence consumed the room. We were both speechless.

I was trying to process it all. Did I know? Could I have known that this horrible thing would happen to me? As a little girl, was I speaking doom over my life? Did this horrible thing happen as a result of my words as a little child? Grandma and I had oh so many talks before. Yet in the course of all those conversations, she never mentioned to me singing that song. I did not know the answer to any of these questions for sure. But like Grandma, I wondered.

We both sat quietly for what seemed like an eternity. I was still trying to process it all. Grandma was still clenching her forehead with her fist as she looked down at the floor. I looked down myself, following her eyes, and flinched at the disgusting metal brace on my leg. I reminded myself to be grateful that I could walk. Indeed, I was thankful, yet I hated the metal brace that was attached to the ugliest string up shoes ever produced in the history of manufacturing shoes.

My shoestrings were untied. While I tied a perfect bow with my right hand in a bent-down position, I reflected on the occupational therapist who treated me at the hospital. I recalled showing her that I could tie my shoes with one hand just as well as any of her former patients. At first, she derided my attempts to tie the laces with one hand. Naturally, that caused my blood to boil. Surprisingly though, my anger at her calmed when I realized her insults about my inability to use one hand angered me enough to not feel sorry for myself and instead to practice until I was good at using one hand. It was months later that the neurosurgeon gave me the final formidable prognosis. Although I would walk with assistance, I would never regain the use of my left hand and arm.

I was devastated, but I persevered. I adopted the Serenity Prayer. It was my source of sanity when everything seemed crazy and impossible. I constantly prayed, "God, please grant me the serenity to accept the things I cannot change, the courage to change the things I can change, and the wisdom to know the difference." Well, as much as I want to, I cannot change any of this. I had to make lemonade out of this sour lemon that life handed me. I was just glad to be alive, and right now, that alone was enough. I could not change things. I just had to hang tough and be grateful. Again, I wondered if I knew as a little child that this terrible thing was going to happen to me. What my grandma told me seemed to suggest as much. Did I somehow speak these bad things into my life? "Oh, my goodness!" I gasped as I suddenly remembered a conversation with my dad as my family ate dinner during one of my weekend visits home, mere months before the shooting on that Thanksgiving Eve.

With college completed, I was teaching and enjoying the freedom of not having to pay back student loans—all thanks to my parents, who paid for my education. I loved spending my money on clothes to my heart's content, something I could not do while growing up. I had just purchased a leather coat and a pair of go-go boots. I was thoroughly enjoying the fruits of my labor. Dad advised me to start saving money rather than buying so much stuff I did not need. I laughed, and jokingly said, "I'm not leaving behind my money for y'all to spend."

He laughed and replied, "The only way we will be able to spend your money is if you died on payday."

Recalling that, I gasped again. I was utterly shocked. I had just cashed my paycheck, and my purse was full of money on the night I almost died. It *was* payday! I almost died on payday. Did our words over that dinner table trigger that? Was I speaking doom over my life again? I wondered if this horrible thing happened as a result of my words. *Nah, that just is not possible,* I thought, trying to assure myself. But for real, could it?

Grandma interrupted my train of thought and broke the silence with another loud sigh as she bounced to her feet and abruptly left the room. Immediately, my mood shifted to delightful anticipation, forgetting the panic that had been enveloping me mere moments ago. I had a feeling I knew what was coming; Grandma was about to soothe my nerves with her delectable homemade cakes and pies.

Just as I thought. With an infectious smile, she came into the room and uttered the words I loved to hear her say. "Have some sweetbread?"

"Yes, ma'am," I gingerly replied with a smile. Grandma pulled out a folding table and set the tray on it. On an ornately decorated porcelain plate lay a slice of lemon meringue pie, and a slice of coconut-pineapple cake. Beside it was a full glass of flavored iced tea. I happily devoured the scrumptious treats before me, silently wishing the cake was chocolate. I decided not to say that because I knew Grandma liked to make the coconut-pineapple cake. It was not my favorite, but it was good. Besides, I did not want to sound ungrateful. The sugar overload induced by these sweet treats lifted my spirits.

Grandma was the wife of a minister. Living a block from my parents' house, she had a strong influence on our lives. She and my granddad set some strict moral rules for my daddy and his four siblings that they had to live by. Of course, these teachings and expectations were also passed on to us. Our family was well respected within our community. My dad was one of the first black businessmen in the community, and he provided well for us. Together with my mom, my two brothers and I were blessed with impeccable nurturing, values, and guidance necessary for living a secure, happy adult life. We lived with great anticipation of productive, wholesome lives.

Grandma was born in the late 1800s. At the time of this visit, I was young, about twenty-one years old, yet I knew enough to be intrigued by her fascinating tales of days gone by. "When I met your granddaddy, he came to visit me ridding a p-re-ty gray horse. We did not have cars back then. Can you imagine?" Some people say they dream in color. Well I, on the other hand, listen in color. I visualized the horse as she talked, but I just could not visualize my granddad riding a horse. I just could not imagine my granddad, the reverend, as a young man, let alone performing the physically intensive task of riding a horse.

One anecdote that particularly repulsed me was when she told me she had to pick cotton, and every person in the family old enough to pick had to pick cotton. As they performed this labor, the babies were placed on a blanket under the shade of a tree. The toddlers were given small tree brushes to chase the snakes away because they would drink the baby's milk when left unattended. Grandma chuckled when I flinched because she knew that I was afraid of snakes. Grandma told me about so many things. I am the oldest child, and for nine years, the only granddaughter my grandma had. My male cousin is three months older than I am.

Grandma needed to get things off her chest. As such, I guess I was the easiest person to talk to. Since I was recuperating and had the time, she talked to me. The more she told me, the more I realized what a brilliant woman she truly was. She was the daughter of a sharecropper. Her dad—we called him "Grampa"—was born the year slaves were freed. Grampa's wife died shortly after Grandma and Granddad were married. Granddad's father had also died by this time, so Grampa met Granddad's mom. To the delightful shock of everyone else, they both developed a liking for each other and soon got married too. Once together, they continued rearing their children. When Grandma told me this, I did not respond because I was embarrassed at the thought that my grandparents were simultaneously stepbrother and stepsister after their parents were married. Grandma had taken out a tin box and took out a few news clippings to show me. One was the obituary of her grandmother, who died at the age of 114.

Grandma and Granddad sharecropped. When she heard of land being sold near the town, she walked ten miles to town to purchase that land and built the house she lived in now. She even worked as a domestic worker for a while. By the time her grandchildren were born, she was a housewife. She was determined to provide all the important cultural experiences to her family that she had observed while working for white people and did her best to make them a reality. Granddad, on the other hand, worked for the county. He was a hard worker and used to give his all to his job. Yet despite that, he would find time to spend with his family. How he found that between all his work is a mystery to everyone. I do remember that once retired, he frequently visited with the other elderly men under the shade tree to share the local gossip. I noted that although women were accused of gossiping, in our small town, elderly men entertained themselves under the shade tree at the local shoe shop to gossip.

My dad, a World War 2 veteran, was about to complete a degree in history at a local university when I challenged their plans by being born. Dad left college and went to work to support their new family of three. He and Mom showered me with love and attention. I soon had to share my parents with a brother and then later, another brother. Dad worked hard to become an expert brick mason. He built a house for our family with his own hands. We moved into it when I was about six years old.

Mom belonged to a church in a town near our home, whereas Dad's family church was in the country. Besides being a brick mason, my dad was also a Sunday school teacher at his church. My brothers and I joined Dad's church when we became of age. He would carry us to it every weekend to be a part of his lessons, where we were treated no differently than any of his other students. Mom joined us two Sundays each month.

Mom loved dressing me up for these. Indeed, I was always well-dressed. She even provided piano lessons for me, thanks to which I became the first musician at our church. I was great at school, too, and made fairly good grades in elementary school. By the time I reached the six grade, I was aware of how the fair-skinned children received preferential treatment. One of the areas where I noticed this the most was in school operettas. For instance, they were the first to be selected for parts in plays and to represent the school as queens, regardless of their abilities. This was the beginning of my awareness of prejudice within our community. For my part, I was "paper sack tan," as an older neighbor called me.

I believe it was at that time I realized that I had to excel academically to achieve in this society. In seventh grade, I barely made the honor roll during the first semester. Our homeroom teacher offered money to the person with the best grades in the next reporting period. I did not get the money, but my grades still improved. During the summer of my eighth-grade year, I promised myself that I would make all As on my report card. I studied incredibly hard, and I did make all As in grades 9 through 12. I graduated as valedictorian of my class.

As I mentioned in an earlier chapter, I was in the high school band. We were a joke, but we performed with pride in the blue and gold wool suits we received when the white high school band got new suits. I finally made the basketball team my junior year and starred on our championship team during my senior year. In my sophomore year, we took French with some juniors. The star football and basketball player was in my class. He liked me, and I liked him back. I was sixteen years old, and Mom allowed me to "take company" with him. However, she restricted my dating to our living room.

We dated throughout high school. He graduated first and went away to the state college, but we kept up our relationship. We dated whenever he was in town. I attended the same college the next year. I was so proud of him because he had a full athletic scholarship and starred in both football and baseball.

It was the fall of 1967. I was a freshman at the state college. Otis Redding and four members of his Bar-Kays band were killed in an airplane crash in December of that year. There was civil unrest throughout the country. Public schools were forced to integrate. By February of 1968, the students at our college attempted to integrate the local bowling alley peacefully.

We marched to the bowling alley, where the police scattered us. Remembering the news reports of people in Alabama being beaten and assaulted with water hoses, I panicked and ran back to my dormitory. But I was so frightened that I could not find the campus and ran the wrong way. I have always been timid and sheltered. I was shaken and called home, hoping it would calm my nerves. I began crying when my dad answered, and I vented to him. I was incredibly shaken and horrified.

On February 8, 1968, unarmed male students were on the hill on campus, protesting segregation. They were peaceful, doing absolutely nothing violent, when state highway patrolmen opened fire on the group. I was in my dormitory, which was located near the front of the campus. When I heard the shots ring out, someone near me yelled, "Oh, no, they are shooting the students!"

I shook my head and innocently said, "No, those were firecrackers." I genuinely thought someone lit a match to an unopened pack of firecrackers. I did not realize guns were capable of firing in rapid succession. Moreover, I could not believe the idea that state highway patrolmen—the government—would kill unarmed, innocent students. However, I could no longer be in denial when I saw students bring the many wounded youths to the infirmary located just behind our dormitory.

We learned the inconceivable fact that three of our students were killed. Three children, barely adults, died at the hands of state highway patrolmen, who should have been protecting them, fired on them. As I have mentioned before, my boyfriend was in that crowd, but fortunately, he was not injured.

Inside our dormitory, we were in an absolute frenzy. With one payphone on each of the three floors, we all managed to talk with our parents, all of whom insisted on getting us home to safety. The campus was on lockdown. We had to wait until the next day to leave. We tuned into the local radio station and were horrified when it made some ridiculous statements about our students. A dorm mate commented the reporter was not telling the truth. I naïvely replied, "I thought the news media had to report the truth." That night, in my dormitory, I learned the lesson that you cannot believe everything you hear, not even on the news.

That tragic event, now known as the Orangeburg Massacre, continues to affect my life to this day. I now wonder if my boyfriend's drinking and irrational behavior toward me resulted from the shooting on campus. Did he suffer from PTSD? After all, he was on the hill with the students who were injured and killed. Conversely, I wondered if it was a familiar sin that passed on to him from another generation, or was it his environment? I asked many such questions of myself, but I received no definite answer. I could merely speculate. Yet I continued to wonder if I spoke tragedy into my life on Grandma's porch when I was just a tot.

Charles Capps, in his radio-based ministry, makes a convincing case. I have also read his book, *The Tongue, a Creative Force*. During one of his radio talks, I heard a teaching on Romans 4:17 about how God calls things that are not as though they were. He used that scripture to explain that God speaks things into existence. I learned how it was the spoken word that created this universe. When God said, "Light be," light was. He changed Abram's name to Abraham, which means father of many nations. Every time Abraham's name was called, it brought forth the creative power of God to make him the father of many nations. These scriptures, along with many others, set a great case for the possibility that I had spoken tragedy into my life.

A Bible study teacher once did a teaching on the importance of choosing words carefully. She warned that thoughts can become words that have the potential to shape our destinies. I have no proof of this connection existing in my case, but I have been extremely cautious ever since. I try to be careful when I speak, never saying anything that I think would invite tragedy. I try to say, "I have been diagnosed with cancer," rather than, "I have cancer." The minor difference between both statements makes all the difference. I cringe every time I hear someone say, "my cancer," or "my arthritis."

A few years ago, I made a conscious decision to speak blessings into my life. When greeted with, "How are you?" I instantly respond with, "I'm blessed." I reasoned that regardless of how I felt, I would say that I am blessed. If I said it enough times, I would begin believing it too. Thus, I would start *feeling* that way as well. Indeed, I eventually start feeling blessed. Merely saying it was enough to remind me of God's blessings during trials.

One day I decided I wanted a dog. I had seen other people in the neighborhood get one and how owning a dog radically changed their lives for the better. I adopted a Chihuahua puppy. I gave him the name Blessings with the hope that it would help me feel blessed. Every time I called him; I was speaking blessings into my life. "Come, Blessings, come here," I would call. I had so many struggles, and I was tormented because of them—sometimes daily due to the pain and heartaches. However, I knew that I had to fake it till I made it. I called Blessings for years. It worked! I am truly blessed. I do believe that this change in the words that came out of my mouth set me up for God's blessings. The more I said it, the more I believed it. Proverbs 23:7 confirms this truth.

The scriptures in Philippians 4:12 admonishes that we be content in the situation in which we find ourselves. I tried my best to be content in the numerous difficult situations I found myself in. That was the survival method I used. I bought those lessons and tried my hardest to learn from them. I am not 100 percent sure about a lot of things, but I am 100 percent sure God is real, and He is alive and working to affect the lives of those who trust Him. His blessings will not always come when we want them to, so we must learn to trust Him and wait. While waiting we can speak blessings into our lives.

God is waiting and listening for repentance, for accepting Jesus as our Savior. He is longing to help each of us and will be with us as we pass through the fire. He is undoubtedly real. How do I know? Because I tried Him, and I know. I learned through tragedy and recovery, and by living above tragedy. Throughout most of my life, I felt like I was drowning as I struggled to keep my head above the water, the tides rising to take me down into their depths. I did everything to ensure my faith remained unshaken. I fully bought the lesson that God is dependable, able, willing, ever-present, and always on my side. Furthermore, besides these things, He is no wimp and no pushover. He is above all a winner, faithful, no respecter of persons, and the same yesterday, today, and forever. I could go on and on about how extraordinary He is. I know this because I tried Him, and He was all that to me—and more. Yes, I know because I bought those lessons every day of my life. I lived those lessons in every fiber of my being. Again, as Mama said, "A bought lesson is a learned lesson."

6

STAYING STRONG IN A CRUEL WORLD

If there is no struggle, there is no progress.

FREDERICK DOUGLASS

Life hurts. That is just how it is. There was a time when I genuinely thought that a dedicated profession of my faith in Christ would end all my troubles. I genuinely thought that if I prayed, lived right, and had enough faith, I would be healed. And believe me, I desperately wanted to be healed! In my quest for answers, I scoured through the Old and New Testaments. Eventually, I stumbled across 2 Timothy 3:12 (KJV), which assured me that "all who will live a godly life in Christ Jesus shall suffer persecution." This helped me to recognize that coming to God does not end my problems but often begins them.

Of course, this is the inverse of what many other people think. Many believe that sickness and calamity are results of sin, thinking that God must be punishing the person for something that he or she or the parents did. According to this school of thought, God is

51

a wrathful Creator who punishes people. If you suffer, then you did something wrong to invoke God's wrath.

Frankly, I find that rationale illogical and offensive. Under that standard, when I think of the calamity, there is no way I am being punished. As a matter of fact, I am outraged when someone makes an insensitive statement about how illness is the result of one's bad or sinful behavior. This argument is nonsensical and needlessly pits people against each other. Statements like that make me want to scream. What about the poor, innocent children in hospitals suffering from cancer and other dreadful diseases? What about the children born with disabilities? None of them did anything to cause them such misfortune. They are just innocent, pure souls who are suffering for reasons unknown to them.

In reference to this is John 9:2, wherein the disciples asked Jesus who sinned, the man or his parents, because the man was born blind. In the very next verse, Jesus explained that neither sinned; it happened so that the works of God can be displayed in his life. This clearly debunks the commonly held idea about suffering people. Jesus healed the blind man to demonstrate the love and mercy of God. Jesus's mission was to show that God is a God of love, not of wrath.

This was the major reason I sought to study God's Word, and I simply was not satisfied unless I was in a church that had a strong teaching ministry. I remember hearing my dad's Sunday school class discuss the scripture in Ezekiel 18:1–4. Briefly, it tells that the parents had eaten sour grapes, and their children's teeth were set on edge. The Lord corrected them, saying that they no longer had cause to use that proverb because the soul of that sin shall die. In other words, each person is responsible for his or her own sins. Each person is responsible for his or her own sins *only*.

I know that superstition is ubiquitous among our people. It was handed down to us from slavery. I have learned that all cultures practiced some form of superstition, which is why I do not dismiss them outright. I also learned that during the spread of Christianity shortly after the crucifixion of Jesus, the Roman government diluted and distorted Jesus's message. They found that they could not kill His message, but they did change it in different ways. Then there was the group that mixed their folk religion with Christianity. Many acceptable practices in major denominations are based on tradition and error. That is reason to study God's Word and have a strong relationship with Jesus so you will not be deceived.

In John 16:33 (KJV), He promised that in times of persecution, when we find ourselves most challenged, we can, "be of good cheer; I have overcome the world." I learned that sometimes healing is simply about living above circumstances and calmly letting Jesus work miracles throughout one's life. Once more, in John 9, the disciples questioned Jesus about why a man was born blind. Like a lot of people, they wanted to know if it was because of sin. Jesus assured them it was to show the glory of God. Amid my personal struggles, I have experienced God's glory, His favor, and His provisions firsthand. It was when I hurt the deepest that God revealed Himself to me. Through my struggles, I experienced God's many miraculous works.

I guess what I am trying to say is that when you find yourself backed into a corner, it is not a weakness of character on your part. Rather, it is a strength. My life has been troublesome, tragic, and painful, but I know that God is real, and He is my fortress. I know this not because somebody told me or because I read it. I know because I lived it. I bought these lessons with the experiences, mistakes, trials, fears, doubts, triumphs, and successes of my life. I bought these lessons just like I bought the house I am in now.

When my cousin's husband was sick, I prayed honestly for his healing. He was a good man, and they had a good life with plans for a bright future. We prayed and prayed, but he passed away. It hurt, but God taught me through that experience that death is the ultimate healer. We prayed for healing. His healing was his rest from the labor on this side.

Years ago my mother told my dad as she prepared him to accept that his 103-year-old mother was in the winter of her life that we, "did not come here to stay." She reminded him that his mother lived a good, long life, and he had to let go. That was a profound lesson for me because I, too, was holding onto my beloved grandmother. That lesson is one I am recalling as I experience health issues with my aging parents. Yes, and with myself. I endeavor to learn from Corrie ten Boom, who said she, "learned to hold all things loosely so God will not have to pry them out of her hand." Now that is trust. That is faith. That is my prayer, my source of strength when I must call 911 when I find them not well. It helps me to keep a level head. When I battled cancer the second time and chemo was too devastating, I surrendered my life to God as I asked Him to show me a different way, or if He were ready to take me, I was ready to go. God answered that prayer. Three years have passed, and I am cancer-free.

With all the disease and mass tragedies in this world, we all need to trust God totally. We need to have faith in the faith we profess to have and not lean on our own understanding. We must hold loosely every aspect of our lives and commit it to God. After all, we live to live again with Jesus. We don't have to understand the why, we just need to trust God. I paid for that lesson. I Bought it!

During my training as a professional, I was taught that we learn through repetition. Again, these lessons are not about what I think. Instead, they are about what I know. Mama was right a bought lesson is a learned lesson. The next section is a twelve-week daily devotional. The goal of the devotional is that through personal confession, study, and action, you will develop a committed life to Jesus Christ. In other words, it is my prayer that you will let go of all your stubbornness and your preconceived ideas that are based on hearsay and tradition. It is my prayer that you will let Jesus change your life. You must surrender to Him through blind faith and trust. I pray that you will read the Bible and find a teaching ministry to attend on a regular basis as you trust God to renew your life.

There were a few objectives behind all this. First, in doing so, you will actively confess before people a personal relationship to the living God. Tell somebody. When Christ changes your life, you will want to spread that good news. Moreover, you will validate your faith through the study of scriptures after completing this devotional. Third, you must regularly fellowship with a Bible-teaching group (church) of your choice. Last, you must show your trust in God through personal decisions to run to Him in times of trouble.

To get started with this, you need to arrange some essential objects. Above all, you need your own Bible. You might want to start with a New Living Translation or another one that is easy for you to understand because that is the most important feature. Color highlighters will also be useful for marking passages in your new Bibles. You will then find them easily as you share your faith and review the passages. You will need a notebook or journal that has room for multiple entries as it is beneficial that you repeat the lessons in it. You will see God work as you date your prayer requests and then record the answers. Plus, you might have sudden thoughts or ideas while going through the Bible that you might want to pen. Each week is grouped to follow for seven days, but you may choose to study for weeks if you desire. These are the lessons I bought. Now that they are here for the world to see, I share my hard-earned wisdom with you.

I feel I need to offer a word of caution. We live in a "microwave society." We have become accustomed to getting instant results. God is an on-time God, who answers in His own time. There are no shortcuts. No magic. His works are supernatural, yet they are not derived through magic. Acts 8:9–24 offers an example. John 10:27 offers the goal of the lessons that follow. The lessons I bought through Proverbs follows.

DEVOTIONAL

BOUGHT LESSONS SHARED THROUGH PROVERBS

A Twelve-Week Study

7

FEAR/SALVATION: THE BEGINNING

WEEK 1, PART 1

First, as mentioned in the previous chapter, you need your own Bible. You might want to start with a New Living Translation or another one that is easy for you to understand. The quoted scriptures in these lessons are from the King James Version of the Bible. Color highlighters are useful for marking passages in your Bible, making them easier to find once you begin sharing your faith. A journal or notebook is beneficial for you to repeat the lessons. Each week's readings are grouped to be enough for seven days, but you may choose to study the lessons as you desire. Please record dates. When recording your prayer requests, be sure to date them and leave space to record their answers. You will, in effect, see God at work in your life. Be creative. Select a section that give you a visual of God's faithfulness in answering your prayers. You will realize that God is everything you need.

Week 1, Day 1: The Fear of God Is the Beginning

The fear of the Lord is the beginning of knowledge: but fools despise wisdom and instruction.

—Proverbs 1:7

The fear of the Lord is the beginning of wisdom: a good understanding have all they that do his commandments: his praise endureth forever.

—Psalm 111:10

During my childhood, my parents taught me numerous lessons and shaped my behavior through fear. To keep me in line, I was told that God would punish me if I dared misbehaved. "God made you," they explained, "and you must be a good little girl because that pleases God." "Be good" was my modus operandi throughout life, even after I moved away from home. As a child, I feared my mama's belt and my daddy's look of disappoint. I loved them so much that I wanted to please them, so of course, I tried to be good.

I grew to understand that my earthly, traditional parents used punishment because they loved me. However, this did not change the fact that I feared punishment, so I eventually made the decision to do the right thing—most of the time. Ultimately, I behaved because I respected my parents and loved them too much to disappoint them.

I guess one might conclude that I grew up fearing God in the same way I feared my earthly father. In any case, I feared God a lot more than my earthly father because I was taught that God was everywhere; He sees all and knows all. This fear of God shaped my belief system. It is how my faith developed. For me, the fear of the Lord was the beginning of my faith. I eventually grew wise enough to love and respect God. The fear of God *is* the beginning of wisdom and understanding. Yet be cognizant of the fact that it is just the beginning.

In church, as I came to know God, I found that fear was the beginning of wisdom and understanding. It was the beginning of everything I needed to live a prosperous life. Yes, that fear matured as I grew older. However, the older I got, the harder it got to be good. There were so many temptations, especially in high school and college. No matter how hard I tried, I could not be good enough, even if I just repeated what I heard; that was the sin of gossip. Sometimes the gossip was so juicy that I just had to spread it. Indeed, even when I tried not to sin in those obvious ways, I would fall to sin anyways. Romans 7:14–25 helped me to understand my spiritual struggle. Romans 6:23 provided the fear that motivated me to keep trying to please my Father, God.

I tried my best to be good, but evil would inevitably raise its ugly head. I realized that even when I trying to be good, I was ultimately a sinner. I learned in church school that because of Adam and Eve's fall in the garden of Eden, I was born with a sinful nature. I could never be good enough. I was separated from God and, therefore, needed a Savior. Jesus Christ died just so I could have a reconciled relationship with God. Again and again they preached that I could never be good enough, that I *needed* a Savior. I needed to accept the Lord Jesus Christ as my Savior. Only Jesus could make me right with God, and through Him, I would have eternal life.

The fear of separation from God is the beginning of knowledge. I was listening to all this but still heard nothing. Like so many, I did not come to Christ when life was wonderful and when I had no hardships on my mind, not a care in the world. Each time my youth leader at church talked to me about conversion (that is what they called it in the 1960s. We did not know about the word "saved" yet), I told her, "Not yet." You see, I was only about nineteen or twenty years old. I was enjoying college life and had plenty of time. I had quite a bit of partying to do. I thought that once I became a Christian, all the fun in life would be over. I was young, so I had plenty of time. Little did I know that my life was about to come to a tragic end in just a few months.

If the God that I feared had not intervened and worked that miracle, I would have gone to hell, separated from God. I received serious injuries that left me paralyzed on the left side. In fact, my left arm is totally paralyzed, and I had to wear a metal brace that fitted me from my left knee into the ugly shoes that supported them. At the age of twenty-one, I had just earned my bachelor's degree from the state university and was making my own money. Suddenly, without warning, I was paralyzed for life. The paralysis did not affect my brain but involved my body's left extremities. The worst part was that potential employers saw only the paralysis.

I was suddenly under-qualified for jobs. "Children have lots of energy. You will not be able to keep up with schoolchildren," explained one principal.

"I am a certified speech therapist, not a physical education teacher," I wanted to say. Speech therapists are itinerant teachers. We drove our cars from school to school. The job required that I walk the students to and from my office or room until they learned their routine, and then sit across the table and work on speech correction exercises. How physical was that? Not at all! If I did not think I could do it, I would not have applied.

Despite that, no one would hire me. They said I needed more education in order to get a job that did not involve children because they supposedly had too much energy. Hence, I called vocational rehabilitation (VR), seeking help with funds for graduate school.

"Where do you want to go to school, Benedict College?" the counselor asked. I naively responded that I wanted to attend the state college. In hindsight, I believe that the VR counselor asked the question to confirm that my voice was that of an African American woman. He should have known that Benedict, although a great school, did not have a graduate school. Based on my response, he denied me services. Still, I did not give up. I continued calling VR until the right person answered the phone. That right person helped me receive funding to go to graduate school. At the age of twenty-five, I graduated with a master's degree.

Life as I knew it had drastically changed. I now knew enough to know that I needed God but had no idea how to receive Him or

His benefits. I went to church and heeded the call for salvation. The preacher said some words to me, and at the end of the prayer, he said I was saved. I was more confused than ever before. "Please, God, help me," I would often pray, "I don't understand." I did not feel any different; I just did not understand. What did they mean when they told me that I was saved? What exactly *is* saved?

While in graduate school, I met some young Christians who witnessed the love of God to me. They told me that God, my heavenly Father, loved me so much that He sent His only Son on earth to die in my place. Therefore, it was possible for me to be forgiven of my sins and have eternal life. I was excited! I grew up in church and Sunday school. I knew about the Bible. I knew the Bible stories, but I finally understood the significance of the sacrifice that Jesus made for me. I now understood that I was born separated from God and that Jesus is the bridge that connected me to God. It finally clicked! God opened my understanding. The words that I read for years at my home church came to life. I finally understood.

Jesus is the only way to God, they patiently and lovingly reminded me. They prayed with me. They answered my questions. The youth who witnessed this picked up a muffin that was fresh out of the oven and said to me, "You can smell this muffin. It smells good, but you don't have proof that it will taste good until you taste it. Likewise, with Jesus, you know about Him from church, but until you accept Him as your personal Lord and Savior, you cannot truly experience His goodness and His benefits. So as with this muffin, I invite you to taste and see."

I did not just taste it by nibbling at it but rather, took a big bite out of it. With all my being, I asked the Lord Jesus to come into my heart and save me. Later that night, I dreamed that Satan was after me. I grabbed a knife and fought that enemy. He was not able to defeat Jesus in me. I woke up with the assurance that I was saved and that the Lord God is good. After this, I bought the lesson that "The fear of the Lord is the beginning of salvation." But salvation *is* just the beginning.

Salvation through Jesus Christ is the beginning of a life of adventure. There was so much to learn about the benefits and blessings available to me as a child of God. Eventually, I learned that Jesus sent His Holy Spirit to live in me to lead me and guide me. I go to Him for direction whenever I need it. In fact, I even ask Him which store has the best bargain when my money is low. He warns me of all kinds of things and people that I then avoid in my life. Yes, He leads and guides me. Salvation is indeed the beginning of life—of living a fulfilled life in Jesus. I bought that lesson, especially after experiencing it firsthand.

Application

Are you ready to walk in wisdom? Have you received Christ as your Savior? Romans 10:9 and 10 says, "Jesus died so that you can have life abundantly." Accept Him in your life today. Right now say aloud, "God, I am sorry for my sins. I don't want to be separated from You. Forgive me for my sins. I thank Jesus for dying on the cross for my sins. I accept Jesus Christ as my Savior. I invite Him into my heart to cleanse me of all unrighteousness." Right now, right where you are, speak to God in your own words. Thank Him for Jesus. Thank Him for sending His only begotten Son to die on the cross so that you might have life. Thank Him for your new life in Christ. Ask Him to lead you to righteous living, so you are eligible to receive the promises of God.

Was your experience like mine, where you accepted Christ as your Savior and made the profession of faith but were ultimately confused about what it meant? Or maybe you invited Christ into your life, but for one reason or another, you have walked away from His benefits? Just know that you can, right now, right where you are, renew that positive relationship with Christ. Just go to Romans 10:9 and 10. Tell God all about it in your own words and ask Him to renew your relationship with Him. Believe me, He will.

After you have made that confession, say it aloud so you can hear it. I encourage you to confess before man at your local place of worship. This confession is just the beginning and will enlighten your understanding as you study God's Word. I encourage you to talk to your pastor as well as attend church and Bible study. If you do not have a church, ask God to lead you to one that teaches God's Word.

I encourage you to love God enough to serve Him and fear Him enough to study His Word. The Word will keep you from sin, and sin will keep you from the Word. God will take care of cleaning you up. Just be willing to read His Word, and let the Word of God cleanse you. You must be willing to yield to the cleansing of God's Holy Spirit, who promises to cleanse you from all unrighteousness (1 John 1:9).

Prayer

Father, I thank You for Your Word. I thank You for the light of Your Word. I pray that Your Word will light my path and lead me out of darkness into Your light. [If you accepted Christ as Savior] Thank You for forgiving me and thank You for my new life in Christ. Lead me in a plain path so that I can enjoy the abundant life promised in Your Word. Amen.

⚜

Week 1, Day 2: A Bought Lesson: Salvation Is Just the Beginning

Scripture Reading: Gospel of John 1:1–51; 1 John 1:1–10

Ask God to guide you with understanding as you read the scriptures. Wait and listen to let His Holy Spirit speak to you. Just be available. God wants to help you understand His Word). Journal your thoughts, feelings, and impressions. This will offer you tangible evidence of your spiritual maturity.

Write Your Prayer Request: Be specific in your prayer as that way, you will recognize God's answer to your prayer. Record answers to prayer, take great notes, and don't forget to record the dates.

⚜

Week 1, Day 3: A Bought Lesson: Salvation Is Just the Beginning

Scripture Reading: 1 John 2:1–29; Romans 6:1–23

Ask God to guide you with understanding as you read the scriptures. Wait and listen to let His Holy Spirit speak to you. Just be available. God wants to help you understand His Word. Write about it daily.

⚜

Week 1, Day4: A Bought Lesson: Salvation Is Just the Beginning

Scripture Reading: 1 Corinthians 13:1–13; 1 John 3:1–24

Ask God to guide you with understanding as you read the scriptures. Wait and listen to let His Holy Spirit speak to you. Just be available. God wants to help you understand His Word. Write.

⚜

Week 1, Day 5: A Bought Lesson: Salvation Is Just the Beginning

Scripture Reading: 1 John 4:1–21; 1 John 5:1–21

Ask God to guide you with understanding as you read the scriptures. Wait and listen to let His Holy Spirit speak to you. Just be available. God wants to help you understand His Word. Write about your experience.

⚜

Week 1, Day 6: A Bought Lesson: Salvation Is Just the Beginning
Scripture Reading: 2 John 1–13; 3 John 1–14

Ask God to guide you with understanding as you read the scriptures. Wait and listen to let His Holy Spirit speak to you. Just be available. God wants to help you understand His Word.

⚜

Week 1: Day 7: A Bought Lesson: Salvation Is Just the Beginning

Scripture Reading: John 3:1–21

Today you will review your written responses to the week's lessons. Now write about your personal salvation experience. Talk about how salvation is or was the beginning for you. Write this down in your journal. How does the lesson in John 3 relate to your salvation experience?

8

GOD STILL SPEAKS

WEEK 2

The first week is designed to cause you to do self-inventory and to make life-altering decisions. This second week will only be slightly easier. Follow these instructions and keep it up; the exercises will soon start getting easier for you. It will become like second nature to you. With that said, here is your plan for week 2.

Week 2 Day 1: A Bought Lesson: God's Word Is Alive, and He Speaks

Yea, if thou criest after knowledge, and liftest up thy voice for understanding; If thou seekest her as silver, and searchest for her as for hidden treasures; Then shalt thou understand the fear of the Lord and find the knowledge of God.

—Proverbs 2:3–5

If any of you lack wisdom, let him ask of God, that giveth to all men liberally, and upbraideth not; and it shall be given him.

—James 1:5

Scripture Reading: Psalm 25

Developing a fear of the Lord was just the beginning for me. My mind, my very soul, yearned to be fed. I was hungry, ravenous for knowledge. I needed to know about this Jesus, this person who died on the cross for me. I read the stories about Him in Sunday school and heard the preacher preach about Him in church, but I needed more. I needed to develop an even deeper understanding. So to that end, I started reading the Bible even more. I read the New Testament with zeal, and this time it had far greater meaning to me than before. It came alive! I visualized the passages. I was reading it with such a different energy that whatever I read manifested right before my eyes.

I began aggressively looking for a home-based Bible study group to attend as there were none at the churches in my community. Eventually, I found one that I thought was promising and began aggressively studying the Lord's Word. I enthusiastically shared whatever I learned with others. I was excited about my newfound Savior. He saved my life, and He washed away my sins. I could not sing enough praises for Him. I could not keep these new feelings and this new information to myself. My heart and mind were bursting with it, and I wanted everyone else to know and feel what I was. I wanted to help everybody I knew. I just wanted everybody to enjoy the security I had in Christ. I witnessed to my siblings and my friends. Admittedly, I had trouble convincing some at first. Fortunately, they eventually understood and received the Word with joy, inviting Jesus into their hearts. I learned that all I needed to do was tell them and Jesus would do the rest.

For the word of God is quick and powerful, and sharper than any two-edged sword, piercing even to the dividing asunder of soul and spirit and of the joints and marrow, and is a discerner of the thoughts and intents of the heart. (Hebrews 4:12)

It is the spirit that quickeneth; the flesh profited nothing: the words that I speak unto you, they are spirit, and they are life. (John 6:63)

The scriptures shown above are from Hebrews and John. While reading them, I felt as if God spoke personally to me. God was opening and expanding my understanding, taking me to whole new horizons. Yes, God was communicating with me! He would impress upon my heart, encouraging me to talk to a person about salvation through Jesus. By doing this, Jesus directed me to minister salvation to people who were in need of His saving message.

My eyes were astonished as I soon saw the Word of God begin to manifest in the lives of people around me. I had personally felt they would reject or ignore my efforts, but instead, they wholeheartedly embraced them. This was surprising to me, making me feel blessed to have had this opportunity. No one told me this would happen, but the more I studied the Word of God, the closer I felt to the Savior. The more I studied, the greater I understood God's Word. Soon, I realized that God had given me a hunger for more. I needed to know more. I needed to *do* more to spread His Word. I prayed that God would enlighten my knowledge of Him and His Word. My prayers had, fortunately, lead me to a church that taught the Word of God, from where I had grown to a point where I was helping others around me embrace the Word of the Lord too.

One day while I was reading James, I read that all I needed to do was ask God for wisdom. Of course, I immediately believed the Word of God and cried out to Him for wisdom. I soon realized I was making significantly smarter choices and wiser decisions. Amazingly, God was not only making me wise while reading the Bible, but I was also making wiser decisions in my everyday life. This was a truly extraordinary experience to go through, to *feel* yourself become wiser within a tiny span of time. Wow, it was such a bonus to have God help me with my daily living. When my money was low, God directed me to the store that had the best prices. (This was long before the Walmart era.)

I must include that I was obedient to God's Word as I understood it. I faithfully tithed to the ministry that fed me and gave generously to others. I was twenty-five years old when I started tithing. I believed God's promises in Ecclesiastes 11:1, that I would receive a blessing for my faithfulness in tithing. My faithfulness in tithing was my act of obedience to God's Word, yet I must admit that the promise of a tangible reward helped motivate me when times were difficult. I listened to many sermons about tithing. I also became aware that there were unscrupulous ministries out there who abused the teaching of tithing for their own personal gains. I counseled many confused struggling people who admitted they could not afford to attend church. I shared with them that salvation is free and that I believed giving was personal, between the person and God, who renders justice in every situation. I similarly shared the scripture in Corinthians 9:6–7: "But this I say, He which soweth sparingly shall reap also sparingly; and he which soweth bountifully shall reap also bountifully. Every man according as he purposeth in his heart, so let him give; not grudgingly, or of necessity: for God loveth a cheerful giver."

Mama taught me early in life that it is in giving that we receive. I thank God I bought that lesson. I gave faithfully and sowed into good ground. I heard God speak and was obedient. I thank God that He knows our hearts and understands our plights. That is because of Jesus, who died to set us free. Buy the lesson, and trust God with your tithes. God does not make you feel guilty when life is a struggle. But God will provide.

God was granting me this wisdom to help me live day by day. I found that if I needed something, I should first ask God for His will in the situation for my decision to be a good one. I soon realized that wisdom and understanding were all mine for the asking. All I had to do was remember to go to God before making my choices. It was right there for me to have. Therefore, now when I pray, I go before God in thanksgiving and praise. After I ask for His forgiveness, I talk to Him about all my concerns. Then I quietly listen to hear a word from Him. Prayer is a two-way conversation. We must always be still and listen to God talk. He yet speaks.

Sooner or later, I receive a reply. Yes, yes, I eventually do hear a word from God. The reply always comes; I just must concentrate and be patient. Now whenever I am about to make a purchase or any other decision, I instinctively ask Him and then patiently wait for His advice. It is always a gentle reply, never commanding. And it is your choice whether you want to follow it. Of course, I am now wise enough to know better than not to. The scripture in 1 King 19:11–13 gives great insight on God's voice. Indeed, we must be still and know God. We must be still so we can hear Him.

He is only a prayer away. He is always there, waiting and wanting us to ask Him. My Bible study teacher taught us that God created us with free will. Although He does not want any of us to perish, He will not force Himself on us. He is not controlling. He wants to let us be, expecting us to be responsible adults. He is always waiting and willing to act on our behalf according to His will for our lives. God knows best because He knows the future. But He also has no desire to act like an autocrat and tell us what to do. But when we accept Jesus as Lord and Savior, He, like a loving father, acts on our behalf. I personally love Psalm 91 that says when I call Him, He will answer. Isiah 65:24 says even before they call, I will answer. Those scriptures offered the assurance that God was alive and working in my life.

The lesson I bought is that God wants me to ask for wisdom, and He is always ready to give it to me to heighten my understanding and enrich my life. I can even say that Jesus is alive and communicates with me on a personal level. He is my personal Savior. Yes, He still communicates with His own. We just need to have the consciousness necessary to trust and obey Him. I know because I bought that lesson. God's Word is still alive, and He continues to talk to us when we make ourselves available to just listen. I thank God for giving me the wisdom to buy that lesson and believe it. "Beloved, believe not every spirit, but try the spirits whether they are of God: because many false prophets are gone out into the world" (1 John 4:1).

A word of caution. It takes time to discern God's voice. But keep trusting Him and persist in prayer. He will work out even your mistakes. Read Romans 8:28. Like me, you will buy some lessons on the way, but eventually, you will discern His voice, and your walk with Him will be a great adventure called life.

Application

Jesus is waiting to talk to you. He is nothing more than a prayer away. Prayer is talking to God and being still. Being quiet and humble before God to allow His Holy Spirit to talk to you. As you develop the wisdom and understanding that only God grants, you will learn to discern the voice of God. Isaiah 55:8–9 reads, "For my thoughts are not your thoughts, neither are your ways my ways, saith the Lord. For as the heavens are higher than the earth, so are my ways higher than your ways and my thoughts than your thoughts."

Nevertheless, at this juncture, it is important that I give you a word of caution: It is easy to want something so badly that we mistake our desires as those of God. Yes, we can mistake thoughts for God. Therefore, it is important for us to overcome our vanity. Right now, I am going through a major disruption in my life. It hurts, but life is like a classroom. Some lessons are harder than others. Some lessons we repeat until we learn. But God! God promises in Romans 8:28 that He will work all things together for our good. I love the promise in Isaiah 45:2 that He will make the crooked way straight. The scriptures helped me through some difficult days. I used those scriptures to help others who were going through trying times. I bought the lesson that God still communicate with us today.

Despite my failures, I take comfort in knowing that God will work all things together for my good. Even my mistakes are covered by his promises in Romans 8:28. It is the best insurance policy in the world. I am still hurting from what transpired, but I bought this lesson. We all live and learn in our own ways. I acknowledge that I am anything but perfect. I am still learning this lesson. These are marks of humility. Nevertheless, during it all, I have the assurance that the living God is in control and will work everything out for the best. After all, He takes no pleasure in seeing any of us suffer. In times like this, I just need to rest in Him.

Prayer

Father, I thank You for Your Word. I thank You for enhancing my understanding. Help me become sensitive to Your leading. Give me a clear judgment to discern so that I will know Your voice. Speak to me, Lord, for I want to know Your voice. Lead me in a clear and plain path in Jesus's name. Amen.

Write Your Prayer Request: Be specific in your prayer as that way, you will recognize God's answer to your prayer. Record answers to your prayer. Take great notes, and don't forget to record the dates.

Week 2, Day 2: A Bought Lesson: God's Word Is Alive, and He Speaks

Scripture Lesson: Isaiah 55:6–12

Ask God to give you the ability to understand as you read the scriptures. Wait and listen to let His Holy Spirit speak to you. Believe God wants to help you understand His Word.

Week 2, Day 3: A Bought Lesson: God's Word Is Alive, and He Speaks

Scripture Lesson: 2 Timothy 3:12–17; Psalm 19:1–14

Ask God to give you the ability to understand as you read the scriptures. Wait and listen to let His Holy Spirit speak to you. Believe God wants to help you understand His Word.

✦

Week 2, Day4: A Bought Lesson: God's Word Is Alive, and He Speaks

Scripture Lesson: John 10:1–14; Isaiah 40:8

Ask God to give you the ability to understand as you read the scriptures. Wait and listen to let His Holy Spirit speak to you. Believe God wants to help you understand His Word.

✦

Week 2, Day 5: A Bought Lesson: God's Word Is Alive, and He Speaks

Scripture Lesson: Genesis 3:6–24; Romans 5:1–21

Ask God to give you the ability to understand as you read the scriptures. Wait and listen to let His Holy Spirit speak to you. Believe God wants to help you understand His Word.

✦

Week 2, Day 6: A Bought Lesson: God's Word Is Alive, and He Speaks

Scripture Lesson: Titus 2:1–15; Galatians 2:1–21

Ask God to give you the ability to understand as you read the scriptures. Wait and listen to let His Holy Spirit speak to you. Believe God wants to help you understand His Word.

❧

Week 2, Day 7: A Bought Lesson: God's Word Is Alive, and Yet He Speaks

Scripture Lesson: 2 Chronicles 7:14–22

On this day, you will review your written responses on each day of the week's lessons. Now write about your personal experience with God's Word. Are you inviting God to speak to you? Explain how the lesson in 2 Chronicles relates to God's Word being alive.

Write Your Prayer Request: Be specific in your prayer as that way, you will recognize God's answer to your prayer. Record answers to prayer, take great notes, and don't forget to record the dates.

❧

9
YIELD TO GOD'S WILL

WEEK 3

On a personal note, Proverbs 3 is my favorite. God started to communicate with me through those proverbs. It was during a time in my life when I did not know if I had the strength to face another day. I had accepted Jesus as my Savior and was reading his Word as much as it was in my power to do so. I asked Him to be the Lord over my life. I asked Him to cleanse me of all unrighteousness. I was trying to do the right thing to the best of my ability. I was trying to live right, yet trouble and struggle were always before me. You see sometimes—in fact often—bad things happen to good people. Nonetheless, I bought quite a few lessons in Proverbs 3.

Read Proverbs 3 in the New Living Translation. Read or listen to it daily this week before each of the lessons.

Week 3, Day 1: A Bought Lesson: Not My Will, But God's Will Be Done

My son, do not forget my law, but let thine heart keep my commands; for the length of days and long life and peace they will add to you.

—Proverbs 3:1–2

Cast not away, therefore, your confidence, which hath great recompense of reward. For ye have need of patience, that, after ye have done the will of God, ye might receive the promise. For yet a little while, and he that shall come will come and will not tarry. Now the just shall live by faith: but if any man draws back, my soul shall have no pleasure in him.

—Hebrews 10:35

Scripture Lesson: Ephesians 5:15–21

My life was a daily struggle. I had changed significantly. I could no longer play tennis, softball, or basketball. I had so many depressive emotions, and I had no clue what I could do with them. I was determined to overcome them. Giving up was not an option, and failure was not a part of my vocabulary. By now, I had enough of God's words in me to know that He was bigger than my problems. The Word of God told me that, and I believe God's Word without a doubt. I want God's best for my life. I believe that God's laws are perfect.

With the tenacity of a bulldog after its prey, I studied God's Word and sought His counsel because in it, I knew I would find His will for my life. Zechariah 3:7 says, "thus says the Lord of host: if thou wilt walk in my ways and if thou wilt keep my charge, then thou shalt also judge my house and shalt also keep my courts, and I will give thee places to walk among those that stand by."

I search for scriptures that encouraged me to look at God's promises rather than my own situation. While talking to God, I was impressed to read Jeremiah 6:16: "Thus saith the Lord, Stand ye in the ways, and see, and ask for the old paths, where is the good way, and walk therein, and ye shall find rest for your souls." The more intensely I sought the Lord, the more scriptures He gave me. At first, I denied the reality that God was communicating with me. Who was

I that the great God of the universe would talk to me? I was careful to ensure that it was God and not my will or imagination.

I pleaded even more for His wisdom and understanding. Finally, I admitted to myself that God was talking to me through His Word. What a mighty God! That knowledge made me run to Him for guidance in every situation I found myself in for I had the assurance that His will was best for me. Amid my hurt, pain, and confusion, I bought the lesson that I should always ask God for His will to be implemented in my life. No matter what I wanted, I learned not to pray for what I want, but rather to pray for God's perfect will for me in that situation.

This Christian path was getting exciting. God was speaking to me, and I was compelled to share it with others. While I couldn't keep it to myself, something within me was churning, making me want to scream about God's mercy and goodness from atop the tallest mountain I could climb. Just like with the muffin in my salvation experience, I wanted my family and friends to taste the goodness of God immediately. I had greater reasons to witness the benefits of walking with God. I wanted to help them avoid pain and suffering. I wanted to save any and all from going through the struggles that I was experiencing. I wanted them to experience the joy of salvation through Jesus. I organized Bible studies in my community. Aware of my limitations, I sought volunteers from the Bible college to teach Bible studies as well. I avidly search for the scriptures and studied God's will for every situation in my life. I tried everything in my own power to walk in it. I prayed diligently for God's help and guidance.

After receiving my advanced degree, I prayed for guidance and favor in finding a job. I could not find one in my hometown or within commuting distance. Consequently, I had to relocate. God opened doors, but it was not where I wanted them, nor what I wanted. Regardless, God provided. I thanked Him for the opportunity to work and did my best on the job. I knew it was God's will for me at that time. Admittedly, I did not understand it fully, but I was thankful that I had a job. I met some interesting people and learned some valuable lessons. I was disappointed, yet I learned that that almighty God knows what's best for me. I enjoyed life and continued to pray.

I bought the lesson. That the best place to be is in God's will. On the job that God gave me, I met two ladies who are still my close friends after fifty-years. One of the ladies came to meet her handsome husband through me. Today they have three children and three grands. They had a beautiful life together before he entered his eternal rest. When we pray, we look at the small picture. However, the fact remains that God knows our future. He sees the big picture and is preparing us. Now, that is more than enough of a reason to pray, "Not my will, but thy will be done."

Application

When are the best opportunities to really study God's Word and live in it? During times of trouble, when it seems that your best is not good enough, in times of despair, when it seems that God is too far away. Yes, even when it seems that He does not hear our prayers. And yes—I will say it—when it seems that God just does not exist. All these are the best chances to dig into His word. The entrance of your word giveth light; it giveth understanding to the simple. (Psalm 119:130)

It is the spirit that quickeneth; the flesh profiteth nothing: the words that I speak unto you, they are spirit, and they are life. (John 6:63) thou wilt keep him in perfect peace, whose mind is stayed on thee: because he truthest thee. (Isaiah 26:3)

Many people say that the Law is Old Testament, and, "Jesus came to fulfill the Law." They, therefore, conclude that we are no longer under the Law. Now let us reason together. The Ten Commandments are moral laws. They are basic laws for survival in a civilized society. Do not kill, do not steal, and do not commit adultery are all essential to the foundations of our modern civilization.

Abiding by these laws will keep you out of trouble. This is not brain surgery. We must obey God's laws because they are the will of God. The Pharisees had so many laws designed to make people's lives miserable. Those are the laws we no longer obey.

Now read or listen to Proverbs 3–7. What insightful lessons have you learned?

Journal them. Include your prayer.

Week 3, Day 2: A Bought Lesson: Not My Will, But God's Will Be Done

Scripture Lesson: Matthew 18:11–14

Ask God to give you the ability to understand as you read the scriptures. Wait and listen to let His Holy Spirit speak to you. Believe God wants to help you understand His Word.

⚜

Week 3, Day 3: A Bought Lesson: Not My Will, But God's Will Be Done

Scripture Reading: Romans 12:1–21

Ask God to give you the ability to understand as you read the scriptures. Wait and listen to let His Holy Spirit speak to you. Believe God wants to help you understand His Word. Write your thoughts.

⚜

Week 3, Day 4: A Bought Lesson: Not My Will, But God's Will Be Done

Scripture Lesson: 1 Peter 4:1–19

Ask God to give you the ability to understand as you read the scriptures. Wait and listen to let His Holy Spirit speak to you. Believe God wants to help you understand His Word.

⁘

Week 3, Day 5: A Bought Lesson: Not My Will, But God's Will Be Done

Scripture Lesson: 1 Thessalonians 4:1–8

Ask God to give you the ability to understand as you read the scriptures. Wait and listen to let His Holy Spirit speak to you. Believe God wants to help you understand His Word.

⁘

Week 3, Day 6: A Bought Lesson: Not My Will, But God's Will Be Done

Scripture Lesson: Colossians 1:9–12

Ask God to give you the ability to understand as you read the scriptures. Wait and listen to let His Holy Spirit speak to you. Believe God wants to help you understand His Word.

⁘

Week 3, Day 7: A Bought Lesson: Not My Will, But God's Will Be Done

Scripture Lesson: Matthew 18:11–14

On this day, you will review your written responses on each day of the week's lessons. Write about your personal experience with God's

Word. Can you, or will you, trust His will? Think about how the lesson in Matthew 18 relates to you telling others about Christ. Are you ready to learn this?

By the end of this week, you must be feeling more compelled than ever to begin telling others about the lessons you have bought. However, remember that God rewards those who practice patience. Do not get ahead of yourself as there is still plenty that you must learn. Continue following these steps in week 4.

Write Your Prayer Request: Be specific in your prayer as that way, you will recognize God's answer to your prayer. Record answers to prayer, take great notes, and don't forget to record the dates.

10

GOD'S FAVOR
IS NOT FAIR

WEEK 4

Please pardon my vernacular, but God's favor ain't fair. No, it is not fair, We cannot earn God's favor. We serve a wonderful God who does more than we could ever ask or think. He loves us and is our provider. I pray that this week you will recognize God's favor. It is not luck. It is God's divine favor.

Week 4, Day 1: A Bought Lesson: Favor Ain't Fair

Let not mercy and truth forsake thee: bind them about thy neck; write them upon the table of thine heart: So shalt thou find favor and good understanding in the sight of God and man.
—Proverbs 3:3–4

But when the kindness and the love of God our Savior toward man appeared, not by works of righteousness which we have done, but according to His mercy He saved us, through the washing of regeneration and renewing of the Holy Spirit, whom He poured out on us abundantly through Jesus Christ our Savior, that having been justified by His grace we should become heirs according to the hope of eternal life.

—Titus 3:5–7

Scripture Lesson: Psalm 30:1–12

In 1974, I completed the requirements and was awarded a master's degree in vocational rehabilitation counseling. I chose that field because I wanted to help people who were dealing with problems like mine. It was a calling that connected with me. Unfortunately, just as before, I was unable to find a job. Ironically, I was told I had too much education.

This made me do some introspection. I was highly educated. However, I also represented the top-three demographics experiencing job discrimination. I was black, a female, and I had a physical "handicap." I was initially frustrated with the situation I found myself in. After all, I had no control over any of this. But after I talked to God about it, I suddenly remembered a book I once read, *Games People Play* by Eric Berne. I developed an even more in-depth understanding of what was happening to me. It was institutional prejudice and discrimination.

You see, a "handicapped" person at that time was thought of as a person sitting on the street with his cap in his hand, begging for someone to hand him or her some change. Nobody thought we could work any "normal" job. I resolved not to give up, and I had to encourage myself every day as I searched for jobs. I could not get angry at my situation; nor could I get angry at the people rejecting me. In other words, I could not hate the players. But that did not stop me from hating the game.

Recognizing the game, I was determined that neither my race, my gender, nor my physical disability would define me. God had granted me the privilege to receive an advanced education. I was physically and intellectually capable of doing the job I applied for. Telling me that I had too much education was a slap in the face. I was determined to prove them wrong, so I set out to prove that I was more than capable of performing whatever job I was applying for. I wanted to prove—perhaps more to myself and my parents than anyone else—that whenever given a chance, I would do a great job. The God that I served would help me. I learned in grade school that I had to be better, so I had practice. I was driven. And with God's help, I was a gifted worker.

I was ready to go wherever He sent me. I knew that I had to do the best job possible because I was experiencing a kind of prejudice that was—and continues to be—surrounded by ignorance. I knew God was bigger than my problems. I prayed for divine favor as I applied for a summer job in Virginia.

With His blessings, I got the job. God also moved to provide me comfortable housing during the summer months that I worked there. I rented a room from a lady in a small town in southern Virginia. As I was getting out of my car at my new home, another car stopped on the other side of the street. I was surprised to see a former coworker step out of it. She was visiting a relative in that town. I immediately recognized God's hand in this as we were almost three hundred miles from our respective homes in opposite directions. We had not even seen each other in more than three years. Yet, despite that, through some extraordinary coincidence, we were on the same street at the same time.

The real miracle in it was that we were just casual acquaintances, the kind who works in the same building and only exchanges a polite, "Hello," whenever paths cross. The fact that we were here at the same time, on the same street, and I was outside of the house was truly extraordinary. Alas, that is how God works! He often works in matters that seem small and insignificant at first sight. But He knows what we need and is always working on our behalf.

That former coworker introduced me to her cousin, who lived nearby. I spent most of my leisure time at her cousin's house after my former coworker left the area as she was on a week's visit. God knew I needed friendship in that distant town. By doing so, He provided a daily refuge. The elderly lady that I lived with had lost her sense of smell. Her refrigerator had a horrible odor emanating from inside. I kept milk and eggs in it but could keep little else. To my dismay, one night as I left my upstairs bedroom to go down the hall to the bathroom, I quickly retreated to my room. A bat was flying toward me!

Dark Shadows was a popular television show at that time. My mind wanted to play tricks on me, implying that Barnabas Collins was about to pay me a visit. I quickly recalled the scripture in 2 Corinthians 10:5kjv : "casting down imaginations and every high thing that exalteth itself against the knowledge of God, bringing every thought into captivity to the obedience of Christ." I reasoned that it was just an ugly bat, not a vampire. I went back to sleep and trusted God as I made it through the nights until the problem was resolved.

God knew that I would encounter those unpleasant things at that house and provided a safe place for me during the day. That was an example of God's divine favor. I praise Him for it. Indeed, I thanked Him because I did nothing to deserve it. I did not even pray for it. Yet He promises in Isaiah 64:24 that "it shall come to pass that before they call, I will answer, and while they are yet speaking, I will hear." Hence, the lesson I bought was that favor is not fair. I did nothing to deserve it. I didn't ask for it. It was just God's goodness and His mercy. I made sure not to forget that.

Application

Acts 10:34 lets us know that God is no respecter of persons. None of us are better than the others. None of us are worthy. We are all born with the sinful nature due to the fall of man that is detailed in Genesis 3. Once we accept Christ as Savior, it is His blood that makes us right with God. We all belong to the family of God. In life, things happen, both good and bad. Sometimes it might look like the bad outweighs the good. I had to struggle to avoid that school of thought. I had to remind myself constantly to trust God and not what I was experiencing.

I smile as I remember that God spoke to me in my deepest despair. I was losing my ability to work. I was losing my income. That was a threat to my independence. I asserted my self-worth through my job. I knew when a person asked me, this paralyzed woman, what do you do? I proudly replied, "I am a teacher." To me, being a teacher implied that I had to be smart. I reiterate that what people think of me was instilled in me during childhood.

How was I going to provide the quality of living that I was accustomed to for myself and my daughter? How was I going to be able to continue to live independently? I wanted to buy a home. I wanted a big house that I could decorate and display my creative abilities that were hindered when I lost the use of the left side of my body. I poured out my heart to God. I told Him of those fears. God told me to read the book of Job. I read it but complained that I did not understand God's message to me. God said, "Read the end." I read the end. This lifted my spirits and offered me the hope that my future would be better than my right now. I felt God was telling me that He was going to bless me as He did Job. He also moved me to read Joel 2:25. Those scriptures lifted me out of the land of lack on the avenue of poor me. I changed my thinking and my professions, and I started to prepare for my blessing. Within months, God started working. All that I asked for God provided. It took listening to God's guidance and walking in faith.

There is much that humans have tried to explain away. That is the reason it is so important to read the Word of God and have a personal relationship with Jesus, to trust Him, and to discern truths. There is no substitute for knowing God in spirit and truth.

God is no respecter of persons. He does not love one group of people more than others; nevertheless, He does work supernaturally to affect the events in our lives. That is what I mean by favor. The loving God is always looking out for us and helping to affect the events in our lives.

Favor is not fair. I learned early on that a fair is a carnival. It usually comes around once a year. If you want fair, go to that carnival. That way, you will surely experience fair. The reality is that life is just not fair. God instructs us in Matthew 5:44 to "love thy enemies and bless them that curse you or hate you and pray for them which despitefully use you and persecute you." God says that if somebody does wrong, we ought to love the person anyway. Now what is fair about that? But God says you must first forgive in order to be forgiven by God. God makes the rules. We must simply obey them. We don't have to understand. We must trust God, knowing that He knows what's best. In doing this, we find favor with God. Because of Jesus, He looks beyond our faults and takes care of our needs. Now that is a massive divine favor. While it is not fair, it is still a blessing.

Please don't misunderstand. God does not intend for anyone to be abused. He wants us to treat others right. Abide by His laws, and at the same time, if you are being abused, know when to walk away and when to make a hasty retreat. Just follow the Golden Rule and expect to be treated that way. The Golden Rule was posted in my classroom when I was a child. It instructs us to treat other people the way we want to be treated.

> For if you forgive men their trespasses, your heavenly Father will also forgive you. But if you do not forgive men their trespasses, neither will your Father forgive your trespasses. (Matthew 6:14–15)

You don't repay evil for evil. That is not fair! It is so easy to return evil with evil. It feels so good now. At least that is what many of us are indoctrinated to believe. But it causes more anguish. God forgives us, so we must forgive each other. As we study God's Word, God opens our understanding. Since God is love, we realize that we must love God and love each other as we love ourselves. It is equally important to seek God's guidance in everything we do. The will of God is the safest place to be. We cannot go wrong when we are walking in His will. We may stumble and even fall, but God will inevitably help us get back up. We only fail when we refuse to get back up.

We must always remember that no matter what the situation, God can turn it around. People commit suicide because they see the situation as hopeless. God's favor can turn it around. Things can be so different in a matter of seconds. God does not give us what we deserve; He gives mercy and grace. He gives undeserved favor. An onlooker might observe God's favor in your life and complain, "It's not fair." If this happens, witness to that person about God's love. Tell the individual that you are walking in God's divine favor. Tell him or her that God knows all, and He will make it all right.

Before the subject comes up, you might want to share a lesson that I am still learning. Bad things happen. We live in a fallen society. We don't know how or when or even why, but God in time will work it all out. In the meantime, we trust Him and praise Him because He promised in Romans 8:28 that He will work it out for our good. Let people know that they, too, can walk in divine favor and experience His wonderful works. There is no coincidence, just God's favor at work. By this point, you will already know enough to witness. Start sharing God with someone you love now.

Prayer

Father God, I thank You for Your Holy Spirit, who is leading and guiding me. Thank You for Your blessings. I am so glad that You favor me. Help me with recognizing Your acts of favor in my life and give me the boldness to share Your goodness with others. Help me love as You love me. I surrender my will to You. I ask You to lead me and guide me. Help my understanding. Help me live Your example of love. Thank you. Amen.

Write Your Prayer Request: Be specific in your prayer as that way, you will recognize God's answer to your prayer. Record answers to prayer, take great notes, and don't forget to record the dates.

⚜

Week 4, Day2: A Bought Lesson: Favor Ain't Fair

Scripture Lesson: Jeremiah 29:11–13

I know this lesson spoke to you today. Write about your hopes and unfulfilled dreams or goals. Tell God about them, and see how God works. When you look back, you will be amazed at how the Lord is moving in your life.

⚜

Week 4, Day 3: A Bought Lesson: Favor Ain't Fair

Scripture Reading: Psalm 103:1–18

Ask God to give you the ability to understand as you read the scriptures. Wait and listen to let His Holy Spirit speak to you. Believe God wants to help you understand His Word.

Write Your Prayer Request: You will see that God answers prayers. Be specific as this way you will have written evidence that God answers prayers.

⚜

Week 4, Day4: A Bought Lesson: Favor Ain't Fair

Scripture Lesson: Hebrews 4:14–16

Ask God to give you the ability to understand as you read the scriptures. Wait and listen to let His Holy Spirit speak to you. Just be available. Believe God wants to help you understand His Word.

⌘

Week 4, Day 5: A Bought Lesson: Favor Ain't Fair

Scripture Lesson: 1 Peter 2:9-10

Ask God to give you the ability to understand as you read the scriptures. Wait and listen to let His Holy Spirit speak to you. Just be available. God wants to help you understand His Word.

⌘

Week 4, Day 6: A Bought Lesson: Favor Ain't Fair

Scripture Lesson: Isaiah 54:17

Ask God to give you the ability to understand as you read the scriptures. Wait and listen to let His Holy Spirit speak to you. Just be available. God wants to help you understand His Word.

⌘

Week 4: Day 7: A Bought Lesson: Favor Ain't Fair

Scripture Lesson: Genesis 39:1–23

On this day, you will review your written responses on each day of the week's lessons. Now write about your personal experience with God's Word your notebook.

⁂

This week must have felt considerably different than the one before. Thinking about prayer and writing prayers will now start becoming a feature of your weekly routine.

11

GOD DESIRES BLIND FAITH

WEEK 5

Week 5, Day 1: A Bought Lesson: God Desires Blind Faith

Trust in the Lord with all thine heart; and lean not unto thine own understanding. In all thy ways acknowledge him, and he shall direct thy paths.

—Proverb 3:5–6

Order my steps in thy word: and let not any iniquity have dominion over me.

—Psalm 119:133

Scripture Lesson: Exodus 13:17–22

Now this is a lesson that I bought at first glance. It was one I really bought! I mean, I know that I know that I know that God talks to people even today, despite what we are told. Yes, God speaks to me. How do I know it is God? Well, 1 John 4:1 warns, "Beloved, believe not every spirit, but try the spirits whether they are of God because many false prophets are gone out into the world." Furthermore, John 10:27 says, "My sheep hear my voice, and I know them, and they follow me."

One phrase you will never hear me utter is, "The spirit told me." What spirit? There are plenty of counterfeit spirits eager to lead you and guide you toward destruction. Therefore, it is so important to have the right relationship with God in order to study His Word, to know His voice, and to ask God for His help in all situations. Each time and in every situation, you must try the Spirit by the Spirit so you will discern the voice of God. Otherwise, an evil spirit might exploit your circumstances and lead you astray.

God has encouraged me and helped me overcome many tough and emotionally challenging events by whispering the scripture of Proverbs 3:5 to me. He was instructing me to trust Him—God—with all my heart in complete devotion. I should not try to figure everything out, either. I do not need to know the how or the why behind everything. I need to feel comfortable in not knowing and wait patiently. All I needed to know is that He is taking care of the problem, and that is it. I just needed to know that God had my back.

You see, God's ways are far superior to ours, which is why we cannot come close to figuring out how He will work in any given situation. We are to trust Him and then wait for Him to act. At this point, you might not know what "trust" even means. Is it not relative? Well, "trust" for me is like flopping down on a chair and expecting it to hold my weight without any consequences. It is like driving down the interstate highway at seventy miles an hour, trusting that the brakes will stop the car when I apply them, trusting that other cars will obediently stay in their respective lanes, and that no one's tires will blow out. That is trust.

God told me to trust Him with all my heart, so I would not lean on my own understanding. To this end, I had a dream when I was young that I believe was inspired by God. I was driving down a narrow street in city traffic. The car that I was driving was an exotic new sports car, much like my ex-husband's car. The entire windshield was covered with a black leather strap that blocked my vision. I drove the car at a high speed through heavy traffic and was able to maneuver the car across town to visit my cousin.

The dream weighed heavily on my mind. Indeed, I wondered why I remembered it so vividly in the first place. And then I realized that God was trying to communicate something to me through it. When I heard myself explain the dream to a friend, the meaning instantly seemed clear. I said I was driving a car that had blinders on it. I was guided through the traffic on a narrow street. I reasoned that God was telling me that He was guiding me. I did not understand the full meaning behind this. Indeed, to this day, I am not certain, but I believe that God was assuring me that all I needed was blind faith. Faith that He was leading me. Faith to just pray and seek His face in all things.

I needed to hear His voice, discern His voice, and let Him lead me. I needed to just trust Him because no matter what, He was guiding me. I did not have to understand why I just had to listen and believe. Isaiah 30:21 says, "And thine ears shall hear a word behind thee, saying, This is the way, walk ye in it, when ye turn to the right hand, and when ye turn to the left."

Now that is love. God knew that I was hurting. God also knew of my stubborn pride and arrogance. I was young and educated, so I was confident I could figure it out. After all, who else would try to figure out God's next move aside from me? I was thinking, *God is going to do it this way or that way.* I was leaning according to my understanding. God, however, just showed me that like a dumb plow mule, I urgently needed to be guided. He knew that I was going to look around and try to do it my way. My way might lead to fear, harm, or just an incomplete task. Through the dream, He was showing me that He had total control of my life and was going to do precisely what I needed, not what I wanted.

When we know God's Word and when we know His voice, we can walk in faith because we know God is leading us. God answers our prayers. I tried Him, which is why I know. It did not happen overnight, but at age seventy, I can look back and thank God for the development of blind faith. Like all people, I must always pray for guidance and the wisdom to understand and discern the voice of God. It is a daily decision, and it is a daily walk. Personally, I bought this lesson through a visual experience. God desires blind faith.

Application

The purpose behind narrating the incident of my dream is not to suggest that you get a book and try to analyze your dreams. The dream that I spoke of earlier happened more than thirty-five years ago. I can still see the dream in my mind's eye. It is seared into my brain, and God has quietly revealed its meaning over time. Even as I wrote this, God showed me the dream. I have had two other dreams that encouraged me during times of extreme despair. Psalm 34:18 says, "the Lord is nigh unto them that are of a broken heart; and save with such as be of a contrite spirit." God loves and cares so much about us.

I completely bought the lesson that God wants us to trust Him so much that we can walk with blind faith. Trust is a process that needs time. The more you know about God's Word, the more trials He will deliver you from. And the more problems He solves for you, the more you trust Him. God says, try Him and see that He is more than trustworthy. Just step out on your faith and trust God. But first, know something about His will in the situation.

Pray aloud. Talk with God. Tell Him of His goodness, praise Him. Ask for forgiveness of any known or unknown sin, repent. Tell Him your needs, request. Express your desire to know Him better. And above all, trust Him more.

Week 5, Day2: A Bought Lesson: God Desires Blind Faith

Scripture Lesson: Hebrew 11:1–10

Ask God to give you the ability to understand as you read the scriptures. Wait and listen to let His Holy Spirit speak to you. Just be available. Believe God wants to help you understand His Word.

⁕

Week 5, Day 3: A Bought Lesson: God Desires Blind Faith

Scripture Lesson: Matthew 17:14–21

Ask God to give you the ability to understand as you read the scriptures. Wait and listen to let His Holy Spirit speak to you. Just be available. Believe God wants to help you understand His Word.

⁕

Week 5, Day 4: A Bought Lesson: God Desires Blind Faith

Scripture Lesson: Hebrews 4:14–16

Ask God to give you the ability to understand as you read the scriptures. Wait and listen to let His Holy Spirit speak to you. Just be available. Believe God wants to help you understand His Word.

⁕

Week 5, Day 5: A Bought Lesson: God Desires Blind Faith

Scripture Lesson: John 20:24–29

Ask God to give you the ability to understand as you read the scriptures. Wait and listen to let His Holy Spirit speak to you. Just be available. Believe God wants to help you understand His Word).

⁕

Week 5, Day 6: A Bought Lesson: God Desires Blind Faith

Scripture Lesson: Romans 10:6–17

Ask God to give you the ability to understand as you read the scriptures. Wait and listen to let His Holy Spirit speak to you. Just be available. Believe God wants to help you understand His Word).

⚜

Week 5: Day 7: A Bought Lesson: God Desires Blind Faith

Scripture Lesson: Psalm 37:1–11

On this day, you will review your written responses on each day of the week's lessons. How does the lesson in blind faith relate to you?

Write Your Prayer Request: Be specific in your prayer as that way, you will recognize God's answer to your prayer. Record answers to prayer, take great notes, and don't forget to record the dates.

12

Godly Wisdom and Understanding

WEEK 6

Alas, we are entering your sixth week. If you are sensing any compulsion to give up at this point, kill it instantly and continue through the lessons.

Week: 6, Day 1: A Bought Lesson: God Gives Wisdom and Understanding When We Ask

Wisdom is the principal thing; therefore, get wisdom: and with all thy getting get understanding. Exalt her, and she shall promote thee: she shall bring thee to honor when thou dost embrace her. (Proverbs 4:7–8)

But the wisdom that is from above is first pure, then peaceable, gentle, and easy to be intreated, full of mercy and good fruits, without partiality, and without hypocrisy. (James 3:17)

Scripture Lesson: 2 Chronicles 1:7–12

I continued to face closed doors. I had trouble finding a job as a counselor or a public-school speech therapist in the area that I called home. I did find jobs in other areas that required relocation. Regardless, I persevered and continued to seek God's guidance. I realized something had to be wrong and asked God for His will in the situation. I prayed, "Not my will, but let your will be done." Despite this, I just could not land a job near my hometown. Determined to work, I finally relocated and signed a one-year contract to work as a public-school speech therapist.

My supervisor was impressed with the quality of my work as well as my work ethics. At the end of my contract, I was always offered a renewal. However, I always refused because there were too many disadvantages to living away from the physical support of my family and friends. I just did not think that was God's best for me. Seeking God's guidance, I analyzed the kinds of jobs that were in demand in the metropolitan area that I desired to work in. After a lot of prayers, I decided to make myself more marketable by getting certified to teach children with learning disabilities.

My specialty was new, and there were lots of openings available. I laughed as I enrolled at the local university. I knew this was God's guidance because going back to school was the last thing I planned to do, and I never intended to teach. A speech therapist, I thought, was the closest I would come to a classroom. Thus, the saying, "We make plans, and God laughs."

While enrolled part-time at the local university, I sought the help of a couple of employment agencies. At one such agency, I encountered a counselor who set me on a course that radically altered my approach to job hunting. After viewing my credentials, he said to me, "You don't have a job because you don't know how to get a job. With your credentials, you must make the kind of impression on the interviewer that if he does not give you that particular job, he will be looking for another job to offer you. You must contact his office so often that when he hears your voice, he will know that it's you. Now you must do this in a positive way and not be irritating." He went on to explain how to handle the interview and then suggested that I apply at the Department of Corrections.

The Department of Corrections was the last place on earth that I wanted to work. Nevertheless, I was so impressed with that counselor's wisdom that I picked up an application to apply there. However, I later put it in the trash because the very thought of working there gave me a headache. After a few weeks of more closed doors, I heard an expression on the Christian radio station that spoke wisdom to my situation: "Sometimes God will back you up in a corner in order for you to do what you would not ordinarily do." At that moment, I was indeed in a corner. I needed a job so I could maintain my independence. I also believed that God was telling me to apply for the job at the Department of Corrections.

I applied for a job in a new program as principal at a maximum-security institution. I interviewed with the selection committee. To my surprise, I did not get the job but was advised to apply for another more suitable position they were about to post in the same program. I applied for the job and was believing God, believing that I would get the job. Honestly, by now I just wanted a job. I heard nothing. I watched as the clock passed the closing hour on the closing date. Disappointed, I walked outside, ready to admit defeat when the phone rang. I was offered a supervisory position, which was a few grades lower than the first job. I was later told that the chairman of the search committee was so impressed with me that although the first job was not a good match for me, he was determined to hire me for that next position. I agreed and took the job.

I worked at the minimum-security facility until I completed my credentials for certification to teach. That was the best job of my career, but it was funded by a government grant that was up for renewal each year. This gave me a lot of anxiety as I needed job security. I had no idea that God used that work experience as a setup for future employability.

I completed the requirements for my certification, which was needed to teach children with learning disabilities. I applied to my state's department of education to add learning disabilities to my professional teaching certificate. Speech therapists are certified to instruct students from kindergarten through grade 12. This, in turn, was coupled with my experience, and I was soon issued a new certificate that included teaching children with learning disabilities in grades kindergarten to twelve.

Armed with this, I applied for a job at a local high school to teach learning disabled children. I was scheduled to interview with the local school district's personnel director. When I arrived for it, we immediately began the interview. During it, I was asked a question along the lines of, "Who do you admire most?" or, "Who was the greatest person who ever lived?" My instant answer was, "Jesus!" The district director's eyebrows rose, so I went on to extoll His greatness and why I chose Him.

I passed that interview and was referred to the school building for the final interview with the school principal. All these steps were becoming tedious for me, but I knew I had to stay patient if I were to make the most of what God has in store. I went to my second interview, which went about as basic as you would expect it to. It was mostly generic. However, that changed while nearing the end of the interview, when the principal looked at my credentials and my physical situation. After going through them, he said, "Since you worked for three years at the state prison's school, I believe you can handle these high school students." And he offered me the job, which I eagerly accepted.

During the academic year, one of the assistant principals said to me that I was one of a few people certified to teach high school children with learning disabilities in the entire state. I thought, *Look at God and His glory!* Because of my God-given wisdom, I was working at one of the most prestigious school districts in the metropolitan area. At that time, salaries there were the second highest in the region. I was one of just six black teachers in a faculty of eighty. One of the others looked at me and said, "You must be smart because they don't hire black people easily." I smiled as I quietly praised Him for giving me the wisdom to take the necessary preparations to get this job. Indeed, as Romans 11:33 says, "O the depth of the riches both of the wisdom and knowledge of God!"

I just continued to praise God for His directions. I would never have chosen to work in a prison or to work as a teacher. But the wisdom of God guided me into that field. I worked as a public high school teacher for the rest of my career. I am so thankful that God gave me the wisdom required to prepare myself for something so new, as well as provide me the understanding to seek a career path that I would not have chosen to do myself. I am acutely aware of the fact that God's wisdom is the most important thing, and with everything else that we are trying to acquire, it is equally important to get understanding. I bought the all-important lesson that God gives wisdom and understanding when we ask.

Application

Where are you in your walk with God? I am not asking where you were. Nor am I asking where you know you need to be. I am simply asking where you *are* in your walk with God? What have you done after you experienced your birth anew? First Peter 2:2 says, "As newborn babes, desire the sincere milk of the word that you may live thereby." You grow your natural body by eating nutritious food. You grow your spiritual body by eating, reading, and understanding the eternal Word of God. God gives wisdom and understanding to all who ask.

If you find yourself conflicted due to closed doors, missed opportunities, or any other reason, then give it to God. Trust Him completely and wholeheartedly. Discern His voice while you pray for wisdom and understanding. Let God guide you. He is always a prayer away, waiting and eager to answer your prayers. Just understand that God's timing is different than our timing, and we can never expect it to be on our terms. Sometimes you must wait. That is probably the most difficult thing to do when you need something urgently. This is the time when you use blind faith and just trust Him. Trust God ask for His wisdom, and let Him heighten your understanding so He can direct you toward prosperity.

Prayer

Father God, in Jesus's name, I yield all of myself to You. Help me understand Your ways. Help me understand Your Word. I pray for wisdom. As I read Your Word, help me grow wiser with my decision-making. Help me apply Your Word and Your wisdom to my daily life. Help me, Lord, to love You more, and please give me a greater desire to cast my cares upon You. Thank You for hearing and answering my prayer. Amen.

Week 6, Day 2: A Bought Lesson: God Gives Wisdom and Understanding

Scripture Lesson: Luke 18:1–8

Ask God to give you the ability to understand as you read the scriptures. Wait and listen to let His Holy Spirit speak to you. Just be available. Believe God wants to help you understand His Word.

❦

Week 6, Day 3: A Bought Lesson: God Gives Wisdom and Understanding

Scripture Lesson: Deuteronomy 4:1–9

Ask God to give you the ability to understand as you read the scriptures. Wait and listen to let His Holy Spirit speak to you. Just be available. Believe God wants to help you understand His Word. Like me, be SMART enough to trust God.

❦

Week 6, Day 4: A Bought Lesson: God Gives Wisdom and Understanding

Scripture Lesson: 2 Chronicles 1:10–12

Ask God to give you the ability to understand as you read the scriptures. Wait and listen to let His Holy Spirit speak to you. Just be available. Believe God wants to help you understand His Word. Write your understanding of how wisdom from God led Solomon to incredible riches. Think about how this might possibly happen for you.

～☙❧～

Week 6, Day 5: A Bought Lesson: God Gives Wisdom and Understanding

Scripture Lesson: Deuteronomy 4:1–9

Ask God to give you the ability to understand as you read the scriptures. Wait and listen to let His Holy Spirit speak to you. Just be available. Believe God wants to help you understand His Word.

～☙❧～

Week 6, Day 6: A Bought Lesson: God Gives Wisdom and Understanding

Scripture Lesson: Jeremiah 5:21–25

Ask God to give you the ability to understand as you read the scriptures. Wait and listen to let His Holy Spirit speak to you. Just be available. Believe God wants to help you understand His Word.

～☙❧～

Week 6, Day 7: A Bought Lesson: God Gives Wisdom and Understanding

Scripture Lesson: James 3:17

Ask God to give you the ability to understand as you read the scriptures. Wait and listen to let His Holy Spirit speak to you. Just be available. Believe God wants to help you understand His Word. Furthermore, write about God's wisdom. Are you ready to attain it? Discuss the steps you will take to acquire it.

Write Your Prayer Request: Be specific in your prayer as that way, you will recognize God's answer to your prayer. Record answers to prayer, take great notes, and don't forget to record the dates.

13

GOD IS THE GREAT "I AM"

WEEK 7

You are finally entering the seventh week. Feeling any different? It is important that you begin expressing any changes you are experiencing in a separate location as well. Sometimes writing these things down confirms any insight we might have and adds to our confidence. Here is your schedule for week 7.

Week 7, Day 1: A Bought Lesson: God Is the Great I Am

For the ways of man are before the eyes of the Lord, and he pondereth all his goings.

—Proverbs 5:21

The eyes of the Lord are in every place, beholding the evil and the good.

—Proverbs 15:3

Scripture Lesson: Psalm 139:1–24

I loved the Lord and was excited about His Word. I wanted more. I prayed to God to lead me to a church where I would get some sound teaching. I soon met a young lady who told me about a home Bible study and a church. I instantly joined both the church and Bible study because I knew that was what God had intended for me to do. There I met many new and dedicated Christians. Since then, I just wanted to live for God, wanting to do the right thing in His and man's sight.

I searched the Bible to understand what was right and what was wrong in God's sight. I heard some Christians testify, "Truly I'm saved, I'm sanctified, and filled with the God-blessed Holy Ghost. I got a mind to run on and see what the end is going to be." Thus, I prayed, "God, please sanctify me." I prayed and cried and struggled to deny my fleshy desires. Even though I was raised in a home with strict moral values and knew right from wrong, I still found myself in situations described by the apostle Paul in Romans 7:15–20:

> Now then it is no more I that do it, but sin that dwelleth in me. For I know that in me (that is, in my flesh,) dwelleth no good thing: for to will is present with me; but how to perform that which is good I find not. For the good that I would I do not: but the evil which I would not, that I do. Now, if I do that, I would not, it is no more I that do it, but sin that dwelleth in me.

The home-based Bible study was a blessing. It was held in the home of a dedicated couple who were only a few years older than my parents. They fed us with the Word as well as with some appetite-quenching soul food as they counseled us on the issues of life. It was in their home that I learned about the greatness of God. This fresh insight gave credence to my childhood understanding that God is everywhere and sees all. I now understood that God is the great I Am.

We studied Psalm 139, where I was introduced to three words that described the attributes of God. The first of these characteristics is *omniscience*—God is all-knowing, and He has universal knowledge. I learned that He knew me before I was formed in my mother's womb. God is *omnipotent*; He is all-powerful. And He is *omnipresent*; He is everywhere, always, at the same time. That new awareness gave me greater determination to serve Him than ever before. Hence, I knew without a doubt that God could heal me. I prayed to the great I Am for divine healing.

Through my experiences and forty-plus years of walking with the Lord, I bought the lesson that there is nobody greater than God. This must be obvious to many. However, simply stating it is not the same as feeling it. He sees all and knows all that I do or have done. Yet He loves me, leads me, and guides me. He forgives me whenever I repent. Moreover, at every opportunity, He blesses me. I know that it is because of the blood of Jesus. There is no way I can be good enough to earn it. Yes, God loves me despite my failures. All in all, I bought the lesson that He is the great I Am. You can do the same as well.

Application

God is everything we need to have in life. He is the great I Am. He is all-powerful, all-knowing, and everywhere. Although He has that power and uses that power in the most loving and supporting way, He also forgives us whenever we ask for mercy. God is long-suffering and does not want us to perish. John 3:16 describes the degree of God's love. He gave us Jesus, who indeed is also the great I Am. Jesus lived and died, sending us His Holy Spirit to live in us to provide the power needed to live the life that is pleasing to God.

Prayer

Father God, in the name of Jesus, I come to you today with thanksgiving and praise because You have all power in Your hands. I want to thank You for blessing me and for looking beyond my faults and supplying my needs. I thank You for the knowledge that You are always with me and in every situation. I give You all my problems. I commit them to You, asking You to help me to trust You more and to realize daily that You are the great I Am. Lord, help me rest in You. Amen.

Week 7, Day 2: A Bought Lesson: God Is the Great I Am

Scripture Lesson: Psalm 51:1–19

Ask God to give you the ability to understand as you read the scriptures. Wait and listen to let His Holy Spirit speak to you. Just be available. Believe God wants to help you understand His Word.

Week 7, Day 3: A Bought Lesson: God Is the Great I Am

Scripture Lesson: Jeremiah 32:19

Ask God to give you the ability to understand as you read the scriptures. Wait and listen to let His Holy Spirit speak to you. Just be available. Believe God wants to help you understand His Word.

Write Your Prayer Request: You will see that God answers prayers. Be specific as this way, you will have written evidence that God answers prayers.

Week 7, Day 4: A Bought Lesson: God is the Great I Am

Scripture Lesson: 2 Chronicles 16:9

Ask God to give you the ability to understand as you read the scriptures. Wait and listen to let His Holy Spirit speak to you. Just be available. Believe God wants to help you understand His Word. Write your understanding of how wisdom from God led Solomon to incredible riches. Think about how this might possibly happen for you.

Write Your Prayer Request: Be specific in your prayer as that way, you will recognize God's answer to your prayer. Record answers to prayer, take great notes, and don't forget to record the dates.

Week 7, Day 5: A Bought Lesson: God Is the Great I Am

Scripture Lesson: Exodus 3:1–15

Ask God to give you the ability to understand as you read the scriptures. Wait and listen to let His Holy Spirit speak to you. Just be available. Believe God wants to help you understand His Word.

Week 7, Day 6: A Bought Lesson: God Is the Great I Am

Scripture Lesson: John 11:17–26

Ask God to give you the ability to understand as you read the scriptures. Wait and listen to let His Holy Spirit speak to you. Just be available. Believe God wants to help you understand His Word.

Week 7, Day 7: A Bought Lesson: God Is the Great I Am

Scripture Lesson: John 8:58

Ask God to give you the ability to understand as you read the scriptures. Wait and listen to let His Holy Spirit speak to you. Just be available. Believe God wants to help you understand His Word.

Moreover, reflect on your understanding of "I Am" What relationship does I Am have to your new life in Christ?

Write Your Prayer Request: Be specific in your prayer as that way, you will recognize God's answer to your prayer. Record answers to prayer, take great notes, and don't forget to record the dates.

14

GOD IS ALL THAT I NEED

WEEK 8

Your week 8 is going to be a lot different from those preceding it. Instead of having a different task every day, you will have to repeat the same thing for most of the week. Psalm 23 is extremely important, and it is important you understand its contents. They are central for you to develop humility.

Week 8, Day 1: A Bought Lessons: God Has All that I Need

For whoso findeth me findeth life and shall obtain favor of the Lord.

—Proverbs 8:35

And I have filled him with the spirit of God, in wisdom, and in understanding, and in knowledge, and in all manner of workmanship.

—Exodus 31:3

Scripture Lesson: Isaiah 61:1

I must say that I learned much about God by listening to my paternal grandmother. She was 103 years old when she went to be with the Lord. Honestly, I was more impressed with her wisdom than her age. She worked as a domestic worker after moving from the countryside farmlands to the small southern town that we lived in. I must have been very young when she worked because as far back as I can recall, she was always at home, taking care of her pa—we called him "Grandpa"—and keeping a beautiful home for her husband, whom we called "Granddaddy."

Granddaddy was a preacher. We called him an "easy preacher" because he was soft-spoken and did not yell and carry on like the average black preacher. Did I say black? Why we were colored at that time. Ignorant people called us names, ugly names. Today I cover those painful memories with the blood of Jesus, at least until a more appropriate time. Those words still hurt as I write this.

I laughed hysterically when I heard about the songs that were sung in our churches in the early 1900s. She told me songs like "Do Ra Me Fa So La Se Do" were harmonized and sung by choirs who could not read. She said hymns were outlined by a person who could read so the choir could sing. I found it amazing that we were still practicing this at prayer meetings. I liked that method of outlining hymns, and I hope it continues. I loved church as a child and miss the songs of those old days gone by.

For instance, if we were to sing "Amazing Grace," the worship leader would read each line of the hymn, and then the choir or congregation would sing that line. They repeated the steps until the entire hymn was complete. During testimony time, some mourning person might sing a song like, "Ain't But Me One, Me One, Me One. It used to be Me Six, Me Six, Me Six." This is because they repeated the countdown of dead siblings until only the one is left. It was used to stir up emotions.

I must admit that when I was young, I thought it was funny. Yet at the same time, I was impressed with the creative abilities of older people. My grandmother was a smart woman. She could read and write as good as any. As such, she and granddad had a vast library of books. My granddad must have been an avid reader too. I guess that is how he prepared himself for the ministry that God called him into. Grandma said that they went to school around the planting season. In the springtime, they had to plant the crop, and in the summer, they gathered crops like peaches, peas, and other vegetables for canning.

However, these were minor crops as cotton remained the major industry. During the fall, they harvested cotton. The children went to school between September's cotton-picking season until the Easter snap signaled planting time in the spring. The Easter snap refers to the cold days before Easter. It is assumed that this proverbial snap ends the cold weather, making it the ideal time to begin cultivating the land.

As I matured, I began looking at the older adults in my church differently. I never questioned if they could read or write. I did not realize that they grew up as children of slaves and were themselves the sharecroppers that I read of in history class. Most of them worked in the fields and were just not given an opportunity to go to school as my grandparents did. I saw them recite poems and outline hymns without reading from the hymnal. They had great memories and committed poems and such to memory.

These recitals were flawless; it was as if they had photographic memories. Indeed, many of them had great memories since that was what they relied on due to their illiteracy. To them, God's Word was so precious that they memorized His scriptures. Most of them had great testimonies about the goodness of God. God dealt with them on a personal level, and they loved and revered the Lord for their part.

On the other hand, many of the preachers were not literate either, but they still preached the Word with a powerful anointing from above. I remember the church's services and revival meetings that I attended with my parents and grandparents. I saw God at work in their lives. As a child, I bought the lesson that God has everything we need in life. I especially loved our church because I saw God working in the lives of older people, especially because of what they had been through. They always sang and shouted to the glory of God. I thank God that my parents, without fail, dragged me to church even when I was old enough to question why we had to go so often.

Application

What do you see as your limitations? Can you read and write? Did you say just a little? Well I have fantastic news for you. God's Word is on audio, and since most people have Smartphones and tablets today, you should be able to download an audio Bible app free of cost. You can finally access a version of the Bible that has audio. So if you can get access to the internet, you can listen to the Bible. You can also get CDs, DVDs, and cassette tapes of the Bible if you would prefer that. All these options are either free or very inexpensive.

We make every excuse possible for not reading God's Word. None of them apply anymore. The Bible is even available in braille for the visually impaired. We are well educated, yet we do not know scripture as our parents and grandparents before us did. We do not walk in the same kind of wisdom as they did. We who profess to know that God is our everything and that He has all that we need must examine ourselves to see if we are walking in the knowledge, in the favor, and in the wisdom of God in all that we put forth our hands to do.

> *Prayer*
> Father God, in Jesus's name, I ask You right now to still my mind, my thoughts, and my actions. I hand them over to You exactly as they are. I need more of You—that is all. I commit my ways to You so that You will establish my thoughts. I ask You to lead

me and guide me in all my ways, so I will walk in wisdom and knowledge. I need this so I can really see You working in my life. Lord, I thank You for Your divine favor in my life. Amen.

Week 8, Days 1–6: A Bought Lesson: God Has All That I Need

Scripture: Psalm 23

If you have not done so already, commit this psalm to memory. Journal daily how the Lord speaks to your heart through this psalm. What does it mean to you personally? You have six days to memorize it if you have not done so already. This is another opportunity to listen to Proverbs 3–7.

Week 8, Day 7: A Bought Lesson: God Has All That I Need

Tell me how the Twenty-Third Psalm relates to the bought lesson God has everything I need. Find the scripture describing Jesus as the "good shepherd," and discuss it as it relates to your present need.

Pray.

15

EMPOWERED TO WITNESS

WEEK 9

Throughout my years of experience, I have learned how crucial it is to witness to friends and family. We need to keep our loved ones at the foremost of our spiritual transformations. We need to help them learn about the Lord as well so that they may rest in Him and enjoy His benefits too. This week will help you understand the value of the practice of witness. I hope it will inspire you to pray for opportunities and for the boldness to share the gospel.

Week 9, Day 1: A Bought Lesson: The Holy Spirit Empowers You to Witness

He who corrects a scoffer getteth to himself shame and he that rebuketh a wicked man getteth himself a blot Reprove not a scorner, lest he hate thee: rebuke a wise man, and he will love thee. Give instruction to a wise man, and he will be yet wiser: teach a just man, and he will increase in learning.

—Proverbs 9:7–9

Give not that which is holy unto the dogs, neither cast ye your pearls before swine, lest they trample them under their feet, and turn again and rend you.

—Matthew 7:6

Scripture Lesson: Psalm 1

In earlier lessons, I frequently talked about the zeal with which I had to share my faith. Once you have tasted the goodness of God and experienced His unconditional love and forgiveness, it is natural to want to share it with family and friends immediately, and then eventually with everyone you meet. I wish it were that easy. In my experience, some were not ready, while others were just not interested. Although I sympathized with the former, the latter was especially disappointing.

Nonetheless, the lesson I bought was that prayer preceded every opportunity to share the Word. Prayer was even necessary to discern who to talk to about Christ. Some people knew absolutely nothing about Christ yet pointlessly argued every point. I realized that either they were armed with years of misinformation based wrong teaching or that the enemy had such a stronghold on them that they refused the truth of the gospel. I prayed that the spirit of God would change their beliefs and their circumstances. To soften their stony hearts and to open their eyes to the truth of the gospel. I prayed that their knowledge would grow. Realizing that the timing for witnessing to that person was not right, I lovingly changed the subject and moved on, always praying for them.

As a young Christian, I did not fully understand Ephesians 6: "that we wrestle not against flesh and blood but against powers and principalities in high places." Before I realized that the person I witnessed was not the problem and that Satan was actually the force behind my failure to reach that person, I learned that I needed to pray and ask God to lead me to persons with whom I could freely converse. To that end, I prayed, and eventually, the Spirit of God answered. He gave me precise instructions, telling me to contact the wife of a church member who was now in prison. I was afraid because I did not know her. I knew that I could contact the wife's in-laws, who would gladly gave me her phone number, yet I did nothing. It was easy to justify that I did not know her, so she might reject me and think I was foolish.

I failed again for I was not as brave and adept as I thought I was. Despite my best efforts, I just could not make efforts to get touch with her. I started to reason, *She does not know me. It would be wrong for me to intrude in her life. Perhaps God intended something else, so I should wait.* A few years later, I met the young lady once again in a Bible study group in a neighboring town. Recognizing that God intended for me to talk to her, I mustered up the courage and approached her. After exchanging pleasantries, I told her that God had impressed on me to seek her out and talk to her a few years ago.

She nodded and said she would be delighted to speak with me. We soon deliberated on the approximate time of my commission from God, and she said, "Oh, I wish you had called me back then. I was going through some particularly difficult times and was praying for a friend to talk to. Just knowing that God intervened and paid heed to my prayers. I wish you had talked to me. Though I understand why you didn't."

I was astounded. Her response caused me to promise God that I would never fail Him in that way again. Despite my earlier mistake, the lady and I became friends and spoke often. Through our conversations, I learned her husband was in prison in another state. Once more, the Lord impressed upon me to write to her husband. This time, I did not allow my feelings of inadequacy to prevent me from abiding by His will. I started writing the letter the first chance I got, and the words seamlessly flowed from my brain, through the pen, and onto the paper. I realized, much to my delight and surprise, God was using me supernaturally to write. Once I was done, I rushed to a mailbox and mailed the letter. A few weeks later, his grandmother sought me out after church to thank me for writing to her grandson. She remarked how God was answering her prayers, and that brought a smile to my face. Together, we rejoiced over what the Spirit of God was doing in his life as well as ours.

Almost forty years have passed since that incident, and the young husband that I wrote to while in federal prison is back home. He has been saved and is singing praises of God's goodness in the senior choir at church. With joy in a way only he can share, he tells everyone about God's eternal goodness. His grandma, mother, and father have all passed on, but he is still carrying on their tradition of service to the "Good Lord," as he himself might say. His wife, my friend, loved him dearly. God answered our prayers. They are now resting from their labors. I thank God for using me to witness Jesus in their lives.

Lead me, guide me, Holy Spirit. That is my prayer. This time, I bought the lesson that God empowers us through His Holy Spirit to get His work done. All we must do is be obedient.

Application

Is it in our natures to defend our positions or to defend a point? Why does it come so instinctively to so many? Some people are not ready to hear or receive the Word. Knowing this, it is a modus operandi for me to assess the situation by starting a conversation with them first. I can discern a person's position by asking some basic questions. If I feel the person is open, then I proceed. If the person has a know-it-all vibe, I simply change or alter the subject and move in another direction because the person is not ready for what I must tell him or her. After all, while it is my duty, it is not my job to witness to him or her. As we grow in Christ, we develop an enhanced understanding of other people, thanks to which we can better spot hindering spirits and become more open to being used by the Holy Spirit.

Prayer: Ask God to give you the boldness necessary to share what you have learned.

Write Your Prayer Request: Be specific in your prayer as that way, you will recognize God's answer to your prayer. Record answers to prayer, take great notes, and don't forget to record the dates.

⚜

Week 9, Day 2: A Bought Lesson: The Holy Spirit Empowers You to Witness

Scripture Lesson: Matthew 7:1–5

Ask God to give you the ability to understand as you read the scriptures. Wait and listen to let His Holy Spirit speak to you. Just be available. Believe God wants to help you understand His Word.

⚜

Week 9, Day 3: A Bought Lesson: The Holy Spirit Empowers You to Witness

Scripture Lesson: Luke 9:1–62

Ask God to give you the ability to understand as you read the scriptures. Wait and listen to let His Holy Spirit speak to you. Just be available. Believe God wants to help you understand His Word.

⚜

Week 9, Day 4: A Bought Lesson: The Holy Spirit Empowers You to Witness

Scripture Lesson: Matthew 13:1–58

Write a brief summary to relate this passage to Proverbs 9:7–9.

⚜

Week 9, Day 5: A Bought Lesson: The Holy Spirit Empowers You to Witness

Scripture Lesson: Hebrews 4:1–16

Ask God to give you the ability to understand as you read the scriptures. Wait and listen to let His Holy Spirit speak to you. Just be available. Believe God wants to help you understand His Word.

⚜

Week 9, Day 6: A Bought Lesson: The Holy Spirit Empowers You to Witness

Scripture Lesson: Ezekiel 3:1–22

Ask God to give you the ability to understand as you read the scriptures. Wait and listen to let His Holy Spirit speak to you. In your own words, what are the key points that relate to witnessing. What is God's personal message to you in Ezekiel 3:17–22?

⚜

Week 9, Day 7: A Bought Lesson: The Holy Spirit Empowers You to Witness

Scripture Lesson: 1 Corinthians 3:1–23.

Write your understanding of verses 6-9.

Write Your Prayer as It Relates to Being Used by God to Witness

Write Your Prayer Request: Be specific in your prayer as that way, you will recognize God's answer to your prayer. Record answers to prayer, take great notes, and don't forget to record the dates.

16

GOD IS ALWAYS IN CONTROL

WEEK 10

Congratulations! You have reached the ten-week mark. You are almost through the whole cycle, with just a few more weeks left to go. This week I share ways I learned that God is always in control, irrespective of anything else.

Week 10, Day 1: A Bought Lesson: God Is Always in Control, No Matter How It Looks

He that walketh uprightly walketh surely: but he that perverteth his ways shall be known. He that winketh with the eye causeth sorrow: but a prating fool shall fall. The mouth of a righteous man is a well of life: but violence covereth the mouth of the wicked. Hatred stirreth up strifes: but love covereth all sins. In the lips of him that hath understanding wisdom is found: but a rod is for the back of him that is void of understanding.
—Proverbs 10:9–13

Scripture Lesson: 2 Timothy 3:1–17

At the age of twenty-one, I received trauma to my head that rendered me paralyzed on the left side, something I have narrated earlier. As of this writing, that was forty-nine years ago. I experienced discrimination and problems that are far too many to list. I prayed a lot and learned to trust God with the difficult things in my life. Indeed, there were times when I was sick and tired of being tired and sick. I was thoroughly discouraged and heartbroken. I was in a lot of emotional and physical pain because I hurt too bad to cry. Indeed, I could not cry. I talked to God and diligently studied His Word. God started to help me understand some things through His Word. Of course, I told you that already.

I remember my Bible study teacher playfully telling us not to pray for more faith while introducing the scripture in James 1:2–3: "My brethren, count it all joy when ye fall into divers temptations; Knowing this, that the trying of your faith worketh patience. To loosely translate it James is telling us to be happy when we have problems because problems build faith and faith builds patience."

Essentially, he said that when we pray for more faith, we are asking God to give us more problems. It was shortly thereafter that I encountered the scripture that explains how to increase our faith. According to Romans 10:17, " So then faith cometh by hearing, and hearing by the word of God." In order to build my faith, I listened to sermons on television, on radio, and in local churches. I chose reputable Bible-based ministries to listen to on tape. I even began listening to a lot of Word-based Christian music. I did this in addition to reading the Bible.

You know, right now, at the old age of seventy, I am going through a lot. It is not killing me, but it hurts nonetheless, causing me to lean and depend on God even more. On days like this, I call to memory an experience I had with God. I was about thirty-seven years old, struggling to go to work every day and then come home and be the supermom to my daughter that I wanted to be. I pleaded to God to heal me and change my circumstances. I remember it clearly, as though it happened yesterday. I was driving to my home in Arlington from the middle school where I taught in Fort Worth, Texas. I tried not to complain as I talked to the Lord about my struggles. I pleaded with Him for some relief. The Lord God gave me an answer to my persistent query. God, with His loving and tender mercy, knew that I was suffering and struggling to keep my mind, body, and soul intact. God knew that I was becoming tired, yet I struggled to maintain my faith.

God said to me as I drove my new, gold minivan home, in these exact words, verbatim, "You see, you have a giant sifter over your head. It is the kind of sifter you use when sifting the flour to make a cake. Just as with the lumps of flour that don't make it through to go into the cake, everything in your life that you can't handle gets caught in the sifter, and I protect you from it. Likewise, everything that is needed to perfect you makes its way into your life. If you can't handle it, then it gets caught in the sifter, and you don't encounter it." *Wow,* I thought, *that is profound!*

Here it was, over thirty years later, and I remembered that sifter as I endured the pain, heartache, and embarrassment of fleeing with an order of protection due to domestic violence from the man that I thought God sent to love me. How could I get into a relationship with someone else who wanted to harm me, despite the unconditional love and endurance I had showered him with. I am a praying person. I follow God's guidance, obediently. I wondered how I could have missed God's will in this case. As my thinking became more rational and less "Poor me, woe is me," I realized that God allowed it so I must ask what He is teaching me. I must then trust Him to work it out.

It was hard. When I left my husband, I left all my belongings. A house full of furniture that I personally paid for. Most of it less than a month old, had to be abandoned. Most of the oldest objects in that house were only about four years old, and there was precious glassware that I had purchased over forty years ago, while in college and shortly after I graduated. I will not pretend to quote scriptures about where my treasure is as there is where my heart lies. But I will confess that it hurts to have left it behind.

During the waiting period, I purposed each day to renew my mind and practice Philippians 4:8 to keep my mind on good things. It was a chore at times, but when I kept my eyes on God and not the situation, I was okay. My mother was hospitalized about that time, and this distracted my thinking. I was displaced for almost a year. The Lord provided! It was amazing how He worked things out. I did things to feed my faith. I read books by Carolyn Leaf to retrain my brain. I found Bible affirmations to read daily in order to keep positive stuff on my mind. I listened to sermons by pastors like Debleaire Snell, and Joel Osteen. I frequently clapped and sang to Kirk Franklin's "Smile" and "A God Like You," and to Bishop Paul Morton's songs. Indeed, there were innumerable gospel songs I listened to. I learned that praise was the best way to defeat depression and negative thoughts.

A so-called friend said that I missed God and then went on to assert her negative opinion about my decision to remarry. It hurt because I needed comfort rather than judgment. I smiled internally because although I was disappointed, I trusted God and was a stronger person after going through the ordeal that she knew nothing about. I realized that it was God's plan to bless both of us. I took nothing from Him. Yet God used my own resources to multiply them. We both walked away from the marriage better off than before. God answered some serious prayers through our brief union. I learned that God is in control. I know by now that His thoughts and wisdom are so great that there is no way I can explain or understand the how or the why of what happens. I learned that He is so wise that He makes no mistakes, and He is so loving that He would never do anything wrong. Through my suffering, I learned that God loves me so much that He sent His Son to die so that I can live. Through all that has happened in my life, this fact keeps me trusting Him.

Bought lesson: We cannot second-guess God. We don't need to understand Him. We just need to trust Him no matter what.

Application

Psalm 37 is powerful. No matter who we are or what circumstances or calamities we face, this psalm speaks personally to each of us and our situations. Whether we are new Christians or if we have been on the battlefield for a long time, it is human nature to feel that our troubles are suddenly over, and because of Christ, our lives will be problem-free moving forward. Quite the contrary; that is when problems arise. In 2 Timothy 3:12, it says, "Yea, that all those who live Godly in Christ Jesus shall suffer persecution." First Peter 5:8 warns us to be careful, to watch out, because the enemy, the one who wants to destroy us, is roaming around, looking for opportunities to wipe us out. It's his job, and he is looking for any and every opportunity. He wants to destroy all those who belong to Christ. He wants us all to join him and his demonic forces.

In other words, before we become Christians, we all belong to the devil. When God created man, He placed them, Adam and Eve, in the garden. He gave them exclusive dominion over everything. Alas, He gave Adam specific instructions that they were free to enjoy everything in the garden with one key exception: They should not eat or even touch a certain tree in the middle of the garden. If they did, they would die. You see, Satan was in that tree. We all know how it goes. Satan manifested as a serpent and tricked Adam and Eve in to disobeying God. Disobedience to God is a sin. Period.

Adam's sin gave Satan power over the world. Since Satan defeated the first Adam, God sent a second Adam, Jesus, who defeated Satan on Calvary's cross. Jesus took back the dominion that Adam gave up in the garden. Satan is a defeated foe, yet he remains determined to take as many souls as he possibly can with him despite that fact. He is still a deceiving foe. He is using the same old tricks that worked before. He is still causing trouble. He is causing hatred among the races. He is causing the haves to belittle and trample on the have-nots (pitting rich against the poor). Domestic violence is now an epidemic. Female teachers now emulate male teachers, preying on unsuspecting students. Little boys are now victimized.

All the while, those who make and enforce the laws, placed in positions of responsibility, act as apathetic bystanders. Pastors are dating male and female parishioners, while their wives suffer in silence. Pastors are even teaching and preaching trickle-down economics all so they can drive luxury cars and live in mansions while their members give, give and give; driven by their wants and needs. Yes, Satan is the deceiving factor in these cases and more.

Satan is the master deceiver. He lies to and accuses Christians all the time. He lies and lies and then lies some more. Regretfully, the worst part is that he uses other Christians to speak his lies when you are going through hard times. This is sad and only happens because of lack of teaching.

I took some time to explain how Satan is the deceiver. But the good news is that Christ won the battle with Satan over you. You became free in Christ the moment you asked Christ to forgive your sins and come into your heart and be the Lord over your life. Because of Christ, you have the confidence that whatever comes into your life—no matter the trial, no matter the trouble—it will pass. That is the bottom line! First Corinthians 10:13 saw me through those difficult times. As a young, single Christian, it was a comfort to know that the missed phone call or other disappointment was for my good. God allowed it to protect me from myself—most of the time.

If you have not done so, invite Christ into your life to be your Lord and Savior. You make one step, and He will make two. This is a great time for you to have a talk with a Bible-teaching pastor.

Write Your Prayer Request: Be specific in your prayer as that way, you will recognize God's answer to your prayer. Record answers to prayer, take great notes, and ᴥ﹏ᴥ yet to record the dates.

Week 10, Day 2: A Bought Lesson: God Is Always in Control, No Matter How It Looks

Scripture Lesson: Genesis 2:1–25

Ask God to give you the ability to understand as you read the scriptures. Wait and listen to let His Holy Spirit speak to you. Just be available. Believe God wants to help you understand His Word.

❧

Week 10, Day 3: A Bought Lesson: God Is Always in Control, No Matter How It Looks

Scripture Lesson: Genesis 3:1–24

Ask God to give you the ability to understand as you read the scriptures. Wait and listen to let His Holy Spirit speak to you. Just be available. Believe God wants to help you understand His Word.

❧

Week 10, Day 4: A Bought Lesson: God Is Always in Control, No Matter How It Looks

Scripture Lesson: Psalm 37:1–40

Write a brief summary. Relate this passage to Proverbs 10:9–13).

❧

Week 10, Day 5: A Bought Lesson: God Is Always in Control, No Matter How It Looks

Scripture Lesson: 1 Samuel 16:14–23

Ask God to give you the ability to understand as you read the scriptures. Wait and listen to let His Holy Spirit speak to you. Just be available. Believe God wants to help you understand His Word. Moreover, think about how you can relate this passage to a bought lesson.

~◈~

Week 10, Day 6: A Bought Lesson: God Is Always in Control, No Matter How It Looks

Scripture Lesson: Romans 12:9–21

Think about what God requires of you. Do you need to pray about this?

~◈~

Week 10, Day 7: A Bought Lesson: God Is Always in Control, No Matter How It Looks

Scripture Lesson: Deuteronomy 28:1–15

Based on all that you have learned, list all the blessings for obedience to God.

Write Your Prayer Request: Be specific in your prayer as that way, you will recognize God's answer to your prayer. Record answers to prayer, take great notes, and don't forget to record the dates.

17

WHAT PLEASES GOD

WEEK 11

I hope these habits are coming naturally to you by now. It has been almost three months since we began this process. God already knows everything about us, yet He loves us anyway. No matter what, His love is unconditional. This lesson challenges our natural reactions. This lesson teaches us the God kind of justice.

Week 11, Day 1: A Bought Lesson: Trying to Do the Right Thing Pleases God

A false balance is abomination to the Lord: but a just weight is his delight.

—Proverbs 11: 1

He that putteth not out his money to usury, nor taketh reward against the innocent. He that doeth these things shall never be moved.

—Psalm 15:5

Scripture Lesson: Proverbs 6:1–19

A close friend asked me to help her borrow some money for something important. I was young and struggling to maintain my good credit rating. I was caught off guard by the request and spontaneously replied, "I'll have to pray about it." Later, I asked my parents about it. They said that it was not wise to mix friendship with money because money has ruined many friendships. If you absolutely must loan money to a friend, never loan any more money than you can afford to give away. This is because you should assume, by default, that you will not get it back. Therefore, if the friend fails to repay, then you can forgive him or her while making a mental note never to do that again. In other words, never loan more than I can afford to lose.

I believed that my parent's advice sounded good, but I wanted to know what the Bible instructed on this issue. So I prayed, and God soon guided me to Proverbs 6. That relieved me of all self-imposed feelings of guilt when I declined the request. Yet I had to muster up the courage to just say no and not worry about my friend's look of disappointment or desperation.

In this new life in Christ, to do the right thing we must just say no to more than drugs. We all know the times when the right thing to do is say no. So let us not be dishonest with ourselves or God, and do what we know we must. We just cannot please everyone. We must please God.

Application

As a young Christian, I wanted to please God so much. I was also deeply grateful to God for the mercy that He showed me when He sent His only Son to die so I can have eternal life. John 3:16 says, "For God so loved the world, that he gave his only begotten Son, that whosoever believeth in him should not perish, but have everlasting life."

I was so thankful to God that I was more than willing to do

whatever was needed to please Him. I searched the scriptures to find out what was right in God's sight. The more I studied, the more I learned, and the more I learned, the more I knew that I was accountable to Him.

James 4:17 helped me understand that I am responsible for what I know. Whoever knows the right thing to do and fails to do it will have committed a sin. Like all Christians, I missed the mark a lot of times. It was those times that I repented and asked God to strengthen me so that I can gain victory over that sin. I bought the lesson that trying to do the right thing pleases God. When I fall short and commit a sin, I feel sorry, confess my sin before God, and ask for forgiveness. Jesus, who knows the intentions of my heart, lovingly pleads my case to the Father.

Write Your Prayer Request: Be specific in your prayer as that way, you will recognize God's answer to your prayer. Record answers to prayer, take great notes, and don't forget to record the dates.

Week 11, Day 2: A Bought Lesson: Trying to Do the Right Thing Pleases God

Scripture Lesson: Galatians 6:7–16

Ask God to give you the ability to understand as you read the scriptures. Wait and listen to let His Holy Spirit speak to you. Just be available. Believe God wants to help you understand His Word.

Week 11, Day 3: A Bought Lesson: Trying to Do the Right Thing Pleases God

Scripture Lesson: Romans 12:21

Ask God to give you the ability to understand as you read the scriptures. Wait and listen to let His Holy Spirit speak to you. Just be available. Believe God wants to help you understand His Word. Additionally, on this day, explain what God is saying to you in the above scripture in your own words.

⚜

Week 11, Day 4: A Bought Lesson: Trying to Do the Right Thing Pleases God

Scripture Lesson: Matthew 5:10–12

Ask God to give you the ability to understand as you read the scriptures. Wait and listen to let His Holy Spirit speak to you. Just be available. Believe God wants to help you understand His Word. List ways you can practice this.

⚜

Week 11, Day 5: A Bought Lesson: Trying to Do the Right Thing Pleases God

Scripture Lesson: 2 Thessalonians 3:10

Ask God to give you the ability to understand as you read the scriptures. Wait and listen to let His Holy Spirit speak to you. Just be available. Believe God wants to help you understand His Word.

⚜

Week 11, Day 6: A Bought Lesson: Trying to Do the Right Thing Pleases God

Scripture Lesson: Ephesians 5:17

This week, think about what God requires of you. Do you need to pray about this?

✦

Week 11, Day 7: A Bought Lesson: Trying to Do the Right Thing Pleases God

Scripture Lesson: Ephesians 4:25–29

How does this apply to you? Do you want to please God? How will you strive to do better? What is the right thing learned in this passage?

18

STEP OUT ON FAITH

WEEK 12

You are here—finally! The final week of this life-changing experience. I hope you are as excited about what awaits you at the end of this process as I am. This week is all about taking that final step needed to receive God's blessings. It is deliberately designed in such a way to give you a jump-start to live as God's victorious Christian.

Before starting your lessons, review your first four weeks of prayer requests written in your journal. Record the answers to each prayer along with the date the prayer was answered. Give praises to God. Review four more prayer requests daily, and in like manner, record your answered prayers. You will have a visual of God's presence among us today.

Week 12, Day 1: A Bought Lesson: God Wants to Bless Us—We Have to Step Out on Faith

Whoso loveth instruction loveth knowledge: but he that hateth reproof is brutish.

—Proverbs 12:1

A brutish man knoweth not; neither doth a fool understand this.

—Psalm 92:6

Scripture Lesson: Psalm 119:97–100

Psalm 119 explains the special rights, advantages, and immunity available to everyone who is wise enough to gain the knowledge and understand the wisdom provided by God through the study of His Word and abiding by His laws. Once a person has experienced the blessings provided through keeping His laws, he or she will naturally desire more. Psalm 34:8 invites us to taste and see that the Lord is good. Who hates the instructions of God after experiencing the goodness of His instructions? The fool is the kind of senseless man who hates being reprimanded by God's Word because of his limited understanding.

Application

I am often reminded of a time when my daughter was young, and I was in a home Bible study cell associated with a Dallas, Texas, ministry. I had recently relocated to the area to make a new and better life for us. I knew that God was my Source. I wanted to buy a home in the suburbs, in a nice neighborhood with a lot of green spaces. Properties like these were expensive back then, just as they are today. The term "white privilege" was not coined at that time, still that best describes the obstacles I faced. In other words, segregation was illegal, but the system was set up to favor one group of people over others.

I learned at my high school classmate had purchased a home in the southern area of the state. I called her, expecting encouragement, but received the opposite. Her experience was unfortunate. She, too, was a teacher. She said she hated the area she lived in. It was a big city. She told me of a time she was stopped by the police on her way home only because she did not look like the people who lived in the suburban area in which she recently purchased her home. My response to her was one of empathy and optimism. I said that I was in northern Texas, in a small Dallas-area community. I then invited her to relocate with hopes of a better experience. I did not allow that conversation to change my resolve. It did enlighten me to the challenges and caused me to research carefully the communities where I wanted to purchase a house. Home ownership was my dream, yet I just could not see how it was possible for me to buy a nice house on my own. I prayed and faithfully studied God's Word.

I believed in prayer. I believed the Word of God. I believed God enough to drive with my seven-year-old child across the country for 1,025 miles to get a job, all with the expectation of a happier and peaceful life. I was afraid of big trucks. I was a timid driver. I was paralyzed on the left side. I only had the use of one hand, my right hand. Nonetheless, I trusted God enough to move that distance. I trusted God to get a great job in a school district during a time when there was chaos over teacher certification. I trusted God easily through those things. I knew how to do that, but I did not know how to believe God for a house. Homeownership was the burning desire of my heart, and regardless of that kind of faith and trust, I did not know how to trust God for a house. It seemed too impossible.

One night at the above-referenced Bible study group, a young man testified that God led him past a house and instructed him to buy it. He talked about acting on God's instructions, and once he was on the path, God opened doors so he was able to purchase the house. I reasoned that the man, who just happen to be white, and I were both teachers. I refused to think about why we were instructed never to discuss salaries. I refused to consider that the reason was that they paid white teachers more than us or that they paid males teachers more than females. I knew that God was my Source. I made the choice to think on that and to trust God's Word in Romans

2:11. It let me know that God does not show favoritism. I logically deduced that if God did that for that teacher, He would do it for me as our incomes were probably about the same.

I started praying, gathering my savings, and checking out my credit score. I also gathered a lot of real estate information to make sure I was prepared and looking in the communities that best addressed our needs. I had unwavering faith and enough common sense to know that faith without works is dead (James 2:14–26).

I must confess I am of the microwave generation. I wanted it immediately. I needed it to fit neatly into our school year schedule. I saw a house and invested earnest money on it. I went through the financing process and even placed my daughter in the community school and prepaid for after-school care. I was walking in faith! I had confessed my blessings to my friends at work. I knew God was going to answer my prayer. I was confident in my faith for God's provision. At last God was answering my prayer. The timing was perfect to coincide with the beginning of the school year. I was praising God and testifying of His goodness and faithfulness.

Indeed, the answer came quite literally in the form of two calls I received. One was on Tuesday morning from the mortgage company, informing me that my loan was denied. The other? Well, the school called me, telling me I could not enroll my child in that school until I had proof of residence in that school district. I had no time to process it all. I had to alter the school and daycare plans I made for my young daughter. School was to start that very week, so I had no time to lose. Characteristically, I changed plans and made the necessary corrections to place my daughter in school and daycare in time for her first day at school.

Despite all the disappointments and challenges I have had to contend with throughout my life, my biggest concern was the embarrassment I felt telling my friends that I did not get the house. Alas, I mustered up the courage to tell them. However, I did not seek a refund for the advance payment for that school due to my embarrassment. I quickly got my daughter reenrolled in the school near our apartment and into another aftercare center.

Well I did not let that stop me. I sought God, praying for open doors and divine favor. A couple of months later, God led me to the development of a few homes that were being renovated for sale. I applied for one and received financing for a home that was in the same community as the house I was denied ownership of just a few months before. I was even able to choose the carpet and wallpaper for this new house that God had provided. "Look at God," I exclaimed. He knew how much I love pink and blue. I selected the perfect blue carpet and pink and blue wallpaper for the dining room. I loved my new house. My furniture matched perfectly. That initial disappointment was only an opportunity for God to show up and bless me. Just before moving into the new house, God provided an opportunity for me to purchase a nice new car. When my parents traveled the 1,025 miles to help us move for Christmas, we surprised them with a new car to drive into our new home with a garage. After this, I firmly bought the lessons that there are blessings we cannot receive until we trust Him fully and believe. We must believe regardless of what we see or think. We must step out on faith because God wants to bless us. Genesis 18:14 asks, "Is anything too hard for the Lord?"

Ask yourself if you can see God at work in your life. Are you trusting Him more? Share the results. Ask God to give you the confidence and boldness to share. Write about your blessings. If you are constantly experiencing lack, this might be a great time to ask God to help you get the education and training necessary to offer increase. Please read Luke 18:18–27. Please journal.

Based on your beliefs right now, today, answer the question, is anything too hard for God? Explain your response.

Write about God's blessings in your life since you started these lessons.

Week 12, Day 2: A Bought Lesson: God Wants to Bless Us—We Have to Step Out on Faith

Scripture Lesson: Genesis 12:1–6

Study what God instructed Abraham to do? How did He respond?

⁓⚜⚜⁓

Week 12, Day 3: A Bought Lesson: God Wants to Bless Us—We Have to Step Out on Faith

Scripture Lesson: 2 Corinthians 5:7

This time, write a brief summary and answer the following questions: Do you walk by faith? What does that mean? What is your resolve for the future regarding your faith walk?

⁓⚜⚜⁓

Week 12, Day 4: A Bought Lesson: God Wants to Bless Us—We Have to Step Out on Faith

Scripture Lesson: Proverbs 2:10–11

When wisdom entereth into thine heart, and knowledge is pleasant unto thy soul; Discretion shall preserve thee, understanding shall keep thee:

It is so important to study God's Word and to discern the heart of God. Sometimes we will miss God, but when we are sincerely seeking God, even in our mistakes, God will work things together for our good (Romans 8:28).

Journal about a time you feared that you messed up, but you witnessed God working it out for good.

❦

Week 12, Day 5: A Bought Lesson: God Wants to Bless Us—We Have to Step Out on Faith

Scripture Lesson: Hebrew 10:35–39

In your own words, write this scripture. What does God require of you? Do you need to pray about this? Do you have any need?

❦

Week 12, Day 6: A Bought Lesson: God Wants to Bless Us—We Have to Step Out onto Faith

Scripture Lesson: Romans 12:2

How does this passage inspire change in you?

❦

Week 12, Day 7: A Bought Lesson: God Wants to Bless Us—We Have to Step Out on Faith

Scripture Lesson: Jeremiah 29:11

How does this apply to you? Do you want to please God? How does this verse inspire you to strive to do better, if at all?

Write your prayer of praise and thankfulness to God for your life.

19

IMPLEMENTED LESSONS

In three words I can sum up everything I've
learned about life: it goes on.

ROBERT FROST

For you to be able to summarize the lessons I bought, you must decide to trust the living God and never give up. There have been many times when I felt like there would never be peace in the valley for me. Despite this, on most days, I try to resist all forms of negativity to affirm that the Prince of Peace rules my life. Instead of having no peace, I remind myself that I know peace very intimately. Although my life is not as great as that of some others, considering all that I have endured, the senior superlatives were the spoken words that formed my destiny. I *am* most likely to succeed. I *am* most likely to make it. Phrases such as these became an important part of my life. I remind myself that success is relative. Believe me, I must constantly remind myself.

Nobody told me that life would be easy, and obviously it was not. During those hard times, I learned to hold onto God's never changing hands. My life has not been what I planned it to be. I now fully realize the clear fact that success is extremely relative. I did not commit suicide when the going got rough and suicide seemed like the best solution. Yes, suicide is the devil's answer to every problem we face. Instead, I asked God to help me make it through the day.

At times, I had to live one day at a time. I had enough faith and strength to make it through just one day. I found comfort in the story about the clock that had a nervous breakdown trying to figure out how it could master the sixty ticks necessary to complete a minute, and then multiply those ticks by sixty to make an hour, and then multiply that by twenty-four to make a day. It was too much to figure out. The clock just took one tick at a time. By doing so, it eventually got the job done. In times of extreme stress, I became that clock.

Proverbs 18:15 asserts that intelligent people are always ready to learn. Their ears are always open to knowledge. In my desperation, I sought knowledge. I researched dozens of books and sought all media sources to gain wisdom and understanding. God soon started to illuminate my mind with understanding. I reasoned that I was suffering so much and that I was so sad that God, the loving God, pitied me and gently spoke to me, just as He did for the psalmist, King David.

Due to a host of factors, I experienced ignorance and prejudice aimed at breaking my spirit. The greatest dilemma of my situation was isolation. None of my peers—not even family members—offered to include me in any of their social activities. For my part, I was too proud to ask. To compensate, I developed telephone friendships with a few long-distance friends.

When adversity came, and it came in every form, I knew that it was not originating from God. I knew that God loved me so much that He sent His Son to die for me. Surely, He was going to bring me through to the other end of whatever challenge I was facing. And He did again and again. I admit I went through a lot. I got tired of going through so much. I got tired of suffering. I got tired of the aches and pain. I got tired of stress. I got tired. Period. How much could I take?

To illustrate how bad things were, here are two stories. Everyone knew of my fear of snakes. I cringed in fear at the very sight of snakes. When I was in sixth grade, I was about to jump off our front porch when I saw a snake crawling by. I yelled hysterically until I lost my voice. My peers came to learn of the incident, after which they called me "Snake" as they teased me about my fear. Snakes and guns have always been sources of fear for me. More than fifty years have passed since that incident on the porch, but it is still difficult for me to write about the snake. Another time, I was driving to work one morning when, after about a mile's drive, I noted that a big black snake was crawling from the front grill onto the hood of my car. It stuck its keen tongue out as it crawled forward onto the front fender toward the windshield on my side. I thought I would lose my mind. I started hearing birds chirp as I sporadically had visual hallucinations of being in a jungle. I had to pray and plead with God to keep my mind intact. Soon I was on the two-lane highway. A pickup was about to pass on the right lane. I had to loosen the tight grip I had on the steering wheel to use my right hand to seek his help. I quickly blew my horn and pointed briefly at the snake on my car. I was careful not to lose control of the car. The driver motioned for me to pull into the median lane. We stopped, he took a shovel out of his pickup and pushed the big snake off my car. He appeared as frightened as I was. He motioned for me to run over it. I struggled to composed myself as I watched it crawl across the highway. I drove on to work. I admit that I still I experience heightened anxiety at the memory of that experience. I must concur with Job in Job 3:25–26, "For the thing which I greatly feared is come upon me, and that which I was afraid of is come unto me. I was not in safety, neither had I rest, neither was I quiet; yet trouble came."

On another occasion, when I was about thirty-two years old, I, my daughter, and a friend were traveling back home on the interstate after shopping for my two-year-old's Christmas toys. A driver lost control of his car and knocked the car I was driving off the highway. His car turned upside down, and mine careened right into it. The windshield of my car crushed into the other car's tires. When I regained consciousness, my hair was inches away from the tire. I was still sitting behind the steering wheel. The other car's tire was where my daughter and friend were sitting. My hair was touching the tire. In a daze, I called my toddler's name.

My friend immediately assured me that she had my baby girl and that she was all right. They both were all right, she assured me. We must get out of here. Good Samaritans climbed down the ravine to help us up the steep hill. They took extra care to help me tread the steep incline. We went to the hospital by ambulance. I had recently been a patient at the same hospital, so I knew how it worked. The nurse who attended me at that time was one of my rescuers. She remembered me because the friend riding with me made me an unusual get-well card that caught the attention of that nurse. Who knew that God would use my friend's artistic abilities to garner the nurse's attention, and that the nurse would offer her number as a witness to the accident?

My friend was cut and had surgery to correct lacerations to her face. My daughter and I escaped with minor scratches. It happened so fast that I have little memory of what and how it happened. I was just thankful to God for sparing our lives. Our survival was nothing short of a miracle. The car that hit me knocked my car down the steep ravine. Trees prevented the other car from landing in the water a few feet away. My car landed almost upside down but sideways on top of the tires of that car. The trees prevented us from plowing into the river and drowning. The other driver lied and, of course, blamed me for the accident. I did not get an attorney. My concern was getting another car as I had one more payment before my car loan was paid off. I was also traumatized and struggled to develop enough of a nerve to drive again.

The drunk driver's insurance company contacted me. They reported that their investigation indicated that their insured was totally at fault. He was driving under the influence of alcohol, thanks to which I was able to get enough money to purchase another car. I was quite happy about that and praised God that it was not worse.

During my struggles with the memory of the nerve-shattering accident, I saw the hand of God. There was no seat belt law or car seat regulations at that time. God protected us. God kept us. That was just one more thing that helped me know the reality of God's protection. I chose to look at it in the positive rather than the negative. At the risk of sounding super-spiritual or super-strong, I must confess that those were trying times. I had to do quite a lot of praying and receive affirmations from the scriptures to make it through those difficult days. I could not afford to nurse my wounds. I had to go to work, so back to work I went. I heavily relied on prayer, and each time I drove, my confidence increased.

There is a delightful quote from *Rocky and Bullwinkle*, a cartoon from my childhood. Bullwinkle said, "I done stand all I can stand, and I can't stands no more." At the time, it caught my attention because of its grammatical flaws. As I matured and faced more adversities, I remembered this exact quote and understood that when things get bad, sometimes you must break some grammatical structure to express the frustration of being at the peak of your limit.

Hence, at the old age of sixty-three, I literally heard Bullwinkle speak those words on my birthday during a doctor's visit. Time stopped. My world, my everything crumbled as I heard the doctor speak the most unthinkable of words, "The test results indicate that you have lymphoma, a cancer of the lymphatic system. It is outside your lymph nodes. We found it by accident as it is on the L3 and L4 of your spine. We believe that is the cause of your back pain."

By this time, reality had completely evaded me. I was locked in cartoonsville with Bullwinkle. "I done stand all I can stand, and I can't stands no more!" I do not know what else the doctor said after that, but he gently nudged me back to reality with his appealing manner. He needed to know when I wanted to start chemo and radiation. I had to think about this seriously. I did not want chemo. Hence, I told him that I would call him about perhaps starting with radiation. He set me up for learning more about the procedure and set up an appointment for radiation.

I successfully completed the radiation treatment, after which I consented to chemotherapy. After completing my treatments, the cancer was in remission. I was optimistic about my future, trusting God as I praised Him for being my all-sufficient God.

I pray that the twelve-week Bible study compelled you to make the decision to invite Jesus Christ into your life to be your Lord and Savior. Or that it inspired you to renew your relationship with Christ. It will be necessary to find a strong teaching ministry with which to fellowship. Be prepared because when you come to Christ, Jesus runs the old man, Satan, out. You must fill that empty place with Jesus because Satan will get help and force his way back into your life if you do not fill your life with the wisdom of God's Word. Read Luke 11:24–26 to learn more about this.

All in all, do not think that coming to Jesus guarantees a life without troubles. Just know that in times of trouble, Jesus is with you. This might be an excellent time to read the poem, "Footprints in the Sand." Remember that it is Satan's job to make you believe that God is not the answer to your dilemma. Now that you have completed this chapter, it is advisable for you to periodically repeat the devotion and compare your writings.

This devotional requires a lot of work, and through it, I hope you can proclaim that God is dependable, able, willing, ever-present, and always on your side. He is no wimp, no pushover, a winner, faithful, not a respecter of persons, and the same yesterday, today, and forever. I could go on and on about His infinite virtues. I pray that your problems will be few. Nonetheless, you will agree with me that a bought lesson is a learned lesson.

I know this because I tried Him, and He was all that and more. Yes, I know because I bought those lessons every single day of my life. I lived through those lessons. Momma was right: A bought lesson is a learned lesson. So please, learn these lessons for yourself.

20

EPILOGUE

It is one of the most beautiful compensations of this life that no man can sincerely try to help another without helping himself.

RALPH WALDO EMERSON

I am now and always will be a perfectionist. That trait has provided me with the fortitude to persevere against the countless struggles I have faced in life. A close friend reminded me many years ago that I am at my best when I am helping others. Her words meant the world to me. I chose teaching and counseling as a profession because I wanted to help.

When I was forty years old, my sixteen-year-old niece died from a brain aneurysm It hurt me more than anything. . I just could not function. I remember crying out to God in anguish. I asked Him to help me understand why it hurt so badly. I cried, "God, I know she is saved; I know she has eternal life. Yet, it hurts. God, please help." I pleaded with Him nonstop, hoping He would soothe my pain. And that somehow, I would awake from this horrible nightmare.

I was deeply troubled by her death, and I grew up afraid of dead people to the point that even as an adult, I avoided funerals. I felt a calling to the ministry to counsel in death and dying. I wanted to become a chaplain and help suffering and grieving people. Despite my fatigue and debilitating physical issues and challenges, I prepared myself for professional certification. I entered a seminary and a clinical pastoral education (CPE) program to prepare myself for ministry.

God used me to plant a church, and I successfully pastored for four years, preparing for the ministry of help. I loved my young niece so much, and her sudden, untimely death was so devastating that I wasted no time in helping others. It was during my CPE training I was required to read *The Wounded Healer* by Henry Nouwen. As I read his book, I was reminded of a song that I played on the piano when I was a child, "If I Can Help Somebody as I Pass Along, Then My Living Shall Not Be in Vain." Mahalia Jackson sang it so beautifully, and it has been stuck in my head ever since. I realized that I was a wounded healer who, through service to others, might be able to help myself.

Of the many amazing things, I read in *The Wounded Healer,* one passage stood out to me. It made me realize that Jesus is the wounded healer and that He understands my deepest hurts and pains. Below is a quote from the book.

Nobody escapes being wounded. We are all wounded people, whether physically, emotionally, mentally, or spiritually. The main question is not, "How can we hide our wounds?" so we don't have to be embarrassed, but "How can we put our woundedness in the service of others?" When our wounds cease to be a source of shame and become a source of healing, we have become wounded healers.

This book helped put my life in perspective. I have helped many people since. At one time, I had a telephone ministry. People referred their friends to me, and I counseled them at length over the phone. As I recall, it was during my greatest struggle. Helping others took my mind off my problems and, if nothing else, helped me realize that I was not alone in my struggle. I would hear myself tell them about God's goodness. Hearing those words strengthened my resilience and helped me remember that God would see both of us through our collective difficulty and strife.

Through ministry, I asked Jesus to use me in all my brokenness and imperfections. Jesus used me, a wounded person, with all my issues and despite my baggage. He used me and continues to use me, this wounded person, to heal the hurts of others. I repeat that I am still under construction; God is still working on me. I keep learning and relearning the same things. Yet, even with all my imperfections, Jesus just keeps using me.

I am seeking counseling as of this writing. Admittingly, as I age, aches and pains make it difficult for me to display the joyful optimism that I projected during my many years of struggle. I want to be stronger emotionally to continue being utilized by God to help the wounded. Of course, I realize that it is also a way in which to sharpen my skills and thereby continue serving God's people. The lesson I bought is that you don't have to be perfect to be used by God. You come to Him confessing your brokenness and imperfections—I am the poster child—ready to give it to Him and to allow Him to take care of you. Yes, Jesus is the wounded healer who can and will heal your wounds, our wounds. I know this because I bought that lesson. These lessons helped me set my life. Mama was right, a bought lesson is a learned lesson. Know that learning is lifelong, it's OK as long as we learn from the Master teacher: Jesus, the Christ.

NOW: It's your turn. Will you learn the hard way, as I did or will your surrender your LIFE to Christ and allow HIM to lead you? It's never too late.   We never stop learning lessons.   Time is drawing to a close on this side of Glory. Where do you stand? Write your answer in your journal. Bought Lessons!

About the Author

Sylvia Moore was severely injured and rendered paralyzed on the left side at the age of twenty-one because of domestic violence. She defied all expectations and returned to work after a nine-month recuperation period. After twenty-two years of service as an educator working in both public and private schools, where she gained professional certification in two states, declining health forced her to retire at the age of forty-five. At the point of retirement, she was an ordained minister in a major protestant church denomination, working toward chaplaincy credentials with the Department of Mental Health. Additionally, she was pursuing a doctorate in pastoral counseling.

More recently, she fought her battle with cancer through a holistic approach using *God's Plan* when chemotherapy was too cataclysmic. She remains active in the field of mental health and is involved in programs that offer training in the provision of care that enhances the quality of life for persons with mental illness. She offers experiential counseling to victims of domestic violence. She is an advocate of plant-based diets.

Her personal experiences with sickness and tragedy; her age; her knowledge of mental, emotional, and physical health issues all give her valuable insight as she shares the lessons that she learned while going through her struggles. She bought the lessons in her life. She proclaims that her unwavering faith in Jesus Christ offers credence to her struggle and renders strength to persevere. In *Bought Lessons,* Sylvia shares her story and the lessons she learned going through her trials.

www.ingramcontent.com/pod-product-compliance
Lightning Source LLC
Chambersburg PA
CBHW071224290326
41931CB00037B/1954